ARCHITECTURE FROM WITHOUT

The MIT Press   Cambridge, Massachusetts   London, England

Diana I. Agrest

ARCHITECTURE FROM WITHOUT
Theoretical Framings for a Critical Practice

This book was set in Sabon by DEKR Corporation and printed and bound in the United States of America.

Library of Congress Cataloging-in-Publication Data

Agrest, Diana.

    Architecture from without : theoretical framings for a critical practice / Diana Agrest.

      p. cm.

    ISBN 0-262-01115-8

    1. Signs and symbols in architecture. I. Title.

NA2500.A42 1991

720′.1—dc20   90-35114

                                      CIP

"On the Notion of Place"
First published in *On Streets*, edited by Stanford
Anderson, MIT Press, 1972.

"Design versus Non-Design"
First published in *Oppositions* 6, Fall 1976.

"The Misfortunes of Theory"
First published by the Institut de l'environnement,
Journees de "Theorie et Histoire de l'architecture,"
June 1974.

"Architectural Anagrams:
The Symbolic Performance of Skyscrapers"
Original version published by *L'Architecture
d'Aujourd'hui*, March/April 1975.
English version published in *Oppositions* 11,
Winter 1977.

"The City as the Place of Representation"
First published in *Design Quarterly* 113–114,
Walker Art Center, Minneapolis, 1980.

"Notes on Film and Architecture"
First published in *Skyline*, Institute for Architecture
and Urban Studies, New York, Fall 1981.

"Architecture of Mirror/Mirror of Architecture"
First published in *Rassegna*, Spring 1983.

"Framework for a Discourse on Representation"
First published as an introduction to *Places and
Memories: Photographs by Roberto Schezen*,
Rizzoli and The Cooper Union, New York, 1988.

"Architecture from Without: Body, Logic, and Sex"
Date of article, 1971–1987
First published in *Assemblage* 7, Fall 1988.

Contents

ACKNOWLEDGMENTS

No work is done in isolation; rather, it is the result of the author's interactions with a number of people. In the case of this book, which includes texts written over a long period of time, the acknowledgments date back to the moment at which the essays were first produced. My intellectual debt to others is great, as the content will demonstrate; there are, however, a number of individuals whose interest and support were particularly important in the development of my work.

First and foremost, I would like to thank Mario Gandelsonas, with whom I have had a continuous dialogue throughout the years, for his interest, belief, and encouragement and for his critical voice—always there when I needed it.

A great part of the work presented here was produced during my twelve-year tenure as a Fellow of The Institute for Architecture and Urban Studies; my thanks to its director, Peter Eisenman. The editors of *Architecture d'Aujourd'hui, Oppositions, Rassegna, Design Quarterly,* and *Precis* offered the conditions for various essays to be developed and published.

The encouragement and belief of my friends and colleagues and the discussions I have had with them through the years are in various ways part of this book. I am indebted to Manfredo Tafuri, Anthony Vidler, John Hejduck, Aldo Rossi, Lynne Breslin, Kurt Forster, Kenneth Frampton, and Antoine Grumbach.

I am grateful to Roger Conover for both his interest and involvement at crucial times in the production of the book; to Mark Rakatansky, who was instrumental in the initial steps necessary for this publication; to Diane Jaroch and Mimi Ahmed for their generosity and professionalism in developing the graphics; and to Melissa Vaughn for her editorial thoroughness. Finally, I thank Sylvia Billisics and Lois Nesbitt for their editorial assistance and Sarah Whiting for her help with the translation from French of chapter 3.

INTRODUCTION

Architecture tends to make an absolute separation between theory and practice, between analysis and synthesis. This difference, however, could be better expressed in the difference between discourses: an analytical, exploratory, critical discourse and a normative discourse. Most theories are developed within the first category, while practice falls into the latter.

Critical as opposed to normative discourse allows for questions to grow, to acquire a depth, to open fields, and not to be stopped short by the normative will trying to find immediate answers. The dialectic relationship between those two discourses, the blurring of the boundaries that define them, is what I am interested in.

A theoretical discourse can be developed in different ways, from a historical or a purely critical perspective, a place that implies a certain distance from practice, a position of pure observation, a maximum distance. A theoretical discourse can also be developed from the position of an architect, the producer of architecture, from a minimum distance, which implies a work on both registers, between the two positions.

There is where I find myself in developing critical work. Criticism is developed from questions for which we have no answers, from a first how to a why, a why that makes us bridge those two kinds of discourses. Critical work is a work of demystification, of deconstruction of ideological notions and texts carried out to advance knowledge on architecture.

Architecture has suffered crisis—ideological crisis, lack of direction—in different periods in history. It was such a period that started me on the development of this work. I could say in that sense that this work is autobiographical, as it grew out of a need to understand the origin, the reasons and substance, of this most recent crisis.

To explore the modes of repression—filtering devices and closing mechanisms that took architecture to the most extreme crisis, the disappearance of its own object—is the purpose of the writings that constitute this book. It is from without architecture that one can take a true critical distance. Outside means *from* the city, *from* other fields, *from* other cultural and representational systems.

This latest crisis was the result of the extreme to which the functionalist ideology was carried. This is best seen in the projects at urban scale where architecture produced either overpowering megastructures, immaterial networks, or portable objects.

The question of the crisis of functionalism was manifested not only in its alleged bi-univocal relationship to form, but also in the simplified mode in which form was related to the overall structure of society, that is, with its economic, political, and ideological levels.

The consideration of architecture as an ideological practice offered a way in which architecture (as a subregion of ideology) could be articulated with the other levels in a more specific way, to gain a better understanding of the conditions of its production.

The case of planning in relation to architecture is a good example; as a political tool it served as an intermediary between the overall ideology and the architectural world. For planners the question of culture was not a concern, whereas urban form, the city, architecture, are not only about culture but are themselves a cultural production. This difference became crucial in understanding the ideological transferences from one field to another.

The complex relationship that exists between the urban condition and architecture becomes a recurrent (if not continuous) question in these essays. The urban landscape is the most important spatial production in this century. We live in an urban culture, a fragmentary culture that transcends the limits established by architecture.

My understanding of architecture as a subregion of ideology seen from the perspective of signification and culture allows a work at the level of form—acknowledging the specificity of the architectural—that transcends the apparent functionalist determinism.

This does not mean that these practices and products are considered as fixed structures with fixed meanings, but rather as an open process, as texts rather than languages, as an open world where objects refer to other objects, always postponing an ultimate meaning, as chains of sense where the subject/object relationship of classic criticism was replaced by a relationship between texts.

Bringing this type of discourse into the urban field has had important and productive effects, one of which is a double displacement, that of the subject and that of the object. The subject is not just an architect but is also a critic working in those two registers, while the object of architecture is displaced from the pure object, building, to the urban dimension.

It is from the city (the unconscious of architecture), from outside, that critical work on architecture is developed. This outside is a place where one can take distance from the closed system of architecture and thus be in a position to examine its mechanisms of closure, its ideological mechanisms of filtration, to blur the boundaries that separate architecture from other practices, from other systems, to question the hierarchical position through which architecture produces this filtering.

The relationship between urban form and architecture had not been thought out theoretically, mainly due to the very frequent confusion between the real object and the theoretical object or object of study, and architects had looked at the city as a product, as a building, from an architectural point of view, through an architectural filter.

If one looks at the city from this architectural point of view, one is confronted with the existence of a "creative subject," the architect who would be creating "urban" architecture as a closed reductive system.

But in dealing with the city—and particularly public places—we face a condition that resists design as a closed system. The city is not the product of a "creative subject," and the place of the architect as such is eliminated. The architect, however, could be a reader, reading the city from different positions, different systems. The architect is now placed in the position of a reader, and architecture is seen as a field of differences, making it possible to deal with a phenomenon of fragmentation and change.

The "axiomatic base" of architecture has been displaced in our century from "Roman architecture" and Vitruvius to the contemporary "urban text."

From the field of differences in which architecture has functioned as a closed system, its relationship to other systems has been one of artistic reference, and for a very long time—and particularly at the beginning of this century—the referent for architecture has been painting. This referent is not productive enough when we approach architecture *from* the urban field. A more powerful referent is film, a complex system that develops in time and through space. We can say that film becomes another (referential) outside *from* which to approach architecture.

The essays in this book are like "links in a chain of sense"; they are the response to questions which in turn open other questions in a chain of discoveries. The thought process does not work in such a lineal fashion, and I do not want to present this work either as preconceived or as a lineal process. Other texts and projects were developed simultaneously and have had an impact that I cannot trace with any certainty, as have memories of places and life experiences attached to them, emotions. There is rarely anything that is purely objective, and theory is no exception.

The architect as critic is an a priori to the architecture rather than the last word in relation to the work. The architect is silent when making the object, for the last word, as Barthes says, is that of the critic. The architect as critic is defying his own silence.

The real voice of the writer/architect breaks through the space, the mask of the critic, as though trying to make evident the work of criticism or theoretical work as part of the work of a critical practice, as another form of creativity.

Si j'avais à imaginer un nouveau Robinson, je ne le placerais pas dans une île déserte mais dans une ville de 12 millions d'habitants dont il ne saurait déchiffrer

ni la parole ni l'écriture: ce serait là, je crois, la forme moderne du mythe.   Roland Barthes

We call *place* the theoretical model that describes and explains certain aspects of the built environment in urban contexts within a given structure. The development of this work, the construction of the theoretical model of place, originated when I was confronted with an urban design project dealing with the renewal of a metropolitan area in decay. The project involved the study of the conditions of the area as a first stage and a design solution as a second stage.

An aspect of this work that was particularly difficult was that of trying to derive a solution in the design phase, the transformation of a large-scale program and the quality of the city itself into a particular configuration. There was no methodology or approach that would account in a comprehensive way for the relationship between the diversity of the problems and richness of the area in question and a formal-physical architectural response.

The existing urban environment presents certain problems that cannot be undertaken with the traditional tools provided by architecture and design methods. The problems of the urban environment that we must deal with today are much more complex and cover other levels than those of merely designing an object. Thus the boundaries defining such disciplines as architecture and urban design must be widened according to those requirements.

This work can be articulated in the form of the following questions: 1. What is the nature of the structures that are able to articulate the notion of place? 2. What is the nature of those pertinent "places" where meaning is produced and made man-

Roland Barthes at Cafe Lipp, Paris, Summer 1973. Photograph by D. Agrest.

ifest? The answer to these questions will make necessary the construction of a theoretical model of place or of the notion of place defined in terms of the specific underlying structures that explain the various configurations of objects and spaces beyond their formal or functional aspects.

Public places are of special interest because they are the most significant elements within the urban environment. They can be seen as modes of signification articulating the urban text. It would be possible to characterize these places as "lumps," as formations that establish their limits by their own internal structure, in which a specific combination of various cultural and social codes may be found. One of the places where this is most strongly manifested is the *street*.

On the Theoretical Practice

There are many ways in which one could approach the street as a subject of study. In this approach, the street as a public place, an urban configuration, brings forth particular issues concerning the social production of sense. In this article I intend to make some remarks on the production of sense in the built environment.

Each critical work, irrespective of its content, implies a theoretical approach, which in turn is dependent on a particular representation of the world. On few occasions is this ideological set made explicit. Thus the real implication of the approach, or its essential differences from other approaches, is usually not made clear.

To render a theoretical instrumentality explicit, from the conception of a theory to its methodological procedures, is of major importance in critical work, particularly at the juncture when this analysis enters the public realm, in order to avoid the ideological effects of such discourse. It is especially important now, when theory in architecture is practically nonexistent and when, paradoxically, there is an enormous amount of analysis which is often of great technical virtuosity but without clear indication of its origin, its ultimate orientation, its role in relation to theory. This article deals with the possibility of developing a theory of the built environment as social production of sense and not with the analysis of a particular case drawn from an already constituted theory, since such a theory has not yet been developed.

The explanation of the structure of this essay is itself an intrinsic and theoretically important part of it.

One must first broach the general problems that arise when undertaking a theoretical work, namely, those concerning the conception of knowledge, a conception that is ultimately inseparable from the functioning of society.

An important aspect of the conception of knowledge underlying the majority of theories and one rarely made explicit is the relation of reality versus thought. It is necessary to consider this duality briefly to reveal the initial philosophical epistemological considerations that underlie the development of a theory.

Louis Althusser's analysis of the different conceptions of knowledge,[1] in its general formulation, may be applied to environmental theories and particularly to those based on an empiricist conception of knowledge.[2] In the approach that Althusser terms empiricist, science is seen as a process that develops between subject and object (out there) and that is based on the operation of abstraction. "To know is to abstract from the real object its essence the possession of which by the subject is then called knowledge." According to Althusser, for the operation of abstraction to be accomplished, the real object must be considered as something that "is made of two real essences, the pure essence and the impure essence, the gold and the dross, or, if you like (Hegelian terms), the essential and the inessential."[3]

In this conception the object of knowledge would be the part of the real object that is called pure essence; the process of knowledge would have as its function the distinction and separation of the two parts composing the real object (the essential and the inessential) and the elimination of the real inessential, leaving the subject in front of the essential part of the real object, which alone assures access to the knowledge of it. In this view, knowledge would be present completely, as a whole (object and process) in the real object. The object of knowledge is present in the real object as the part that Althusser calls "the pure essence." The process of knowledge would also be present in the real object as the difference between its two parts, one of which, the inessential, hides and envelops the essential—"*This investment of knowledge, conceived as a real part of the real object, in the real structure of the real object, is what constitutes the specific problematic of the empiricist conception of knowledge.*"[4]

This conception of knowledge recognizes in some way that the object of knowledge is not identical to the real object, is only part of the real. However, while this difference is recognized, the object of knowledge remains obscure inasmuch as it is seen as a distinction between two parts of the same object. In this way the difference between two different objects, between the real object that exists outside the subject and the object of knowledge, is hidden and confused. "This difference should not only be established concerning the object but also between the different processes which should be considered as processes of production, namely, the transformation of a given primary matter (raw material) into a given product by means of the application of given means of production."[5]

As Althusser says: "While the production process of a given real object, a given real-concrete totality (e.g., a given historical nation) takes place entirely in the real and is carried out according to the real order of *real* genesis . . . , the production process of the object of knowledge takes place entirely in knowledge and is carried out according to *a different order*, in which the thought categories which 'reproduce' the real categories do *not* occupy the same place as they do in the order of real historical genesis, but quite different places assigned them by their function in the production process of the object of knowledge."[6]

This implies that knowledge is not a process that is developed between a subject and an object (the world) but is the "definite system of conditions of theoretical practice [which] assigns any given thinking subject [individual] its place and function in the production of knowledge."[7] This production of knowledge can be considered a theoretical practice in that it puts into operation theoretical means of production—a theory and a method—that are applied to a given raw material in order to produce concepts within given historical—theoretical, ideological, economic—relations.

Empiricism is based on an operation of reflection, on building a model of the real. In empiricism, reality and knowledge appear as equal and in this way the production of knowledge remains hidden. This approach implies an acceptance of a reality as it is given and it does not postulate any kind of questioning. It is of interest to recall some examples from the history of science such as those Babylonic instruments for navigation that reflected the position of the stars but did not explain their movements, nor the laws by which they moved, since (at that date) such concepts remained undeveloped. Then there is the example of Copernicus and Galileo in their fight to gain acceptance for concepts contrary to visual evidence; ideas that denied the whole ideology of the church. How was it possible that the earth was not the center of the universe and that it was not the sun that moved around it if that is what they saw? How was it possible that celestial bodies (such as the moon) could be matter? Giordano Bruno was burned by the church. Galileo was imprisoned. The commonsense argument used at the time evoked a disjunction between what was seen and a logic of explanation that was not solely dependent on visual evidence.[8]

It should be remembered that theory "far from reflecting the immediate data of everyday experience and practice can only be constituted through challenging such data, to the extent that its results, once achieved, appear to contradict the experimental evidence of everyday practice rather than reflect it."[9]

An intrinsic characteristic of the ideology of architecture and urban planning is the reflection, rather than the challenge, of reality. Architectural theory should arise from a dialectical relationship to architectural ideology, yet should maintain a degree of radical opposition.

At the present time, architectural theory needs to be developed. It is necessary to acknowledge the critical nature of the two forms of raw material to be analyzed—the given general ideology and the urban environment itself. The means for theoretical production—concepts drawn from historical dialectical materialism and semiotics—and the different stages of analytical procedures must also be studied in the formulation of theory. The critical analysis of the ideological texts, revealing the nature of the ideological obstacle, thus allows for the development of theoretical models with which the urban environment may be considered in relation to culture, as a signifying system.[10]

These models may be applied to the analysis of a second type of raw material—the street. For my purposes, the street is considered as a complex semiotic text, entering the theoretical process in order to produce concrete concepts.[11] It is clear that the issue is neither the description of the concrete nor the knowledge to be abstracted from a real street. Rather the complex process of production of the object of knowledge—the built environment as a production of significance—must provide the basis for further study.

Criticism of the Communications Ideology: Communication/Signification

A work that deals with signification in the environment is linked inexorably to certain practices within the environment (architecture, urban design, urban planning) and thereby necessitates the use of some of the notions that appear in those practices. For this reason, I will deal initially with texts that approach the urban problem through one of the more advanced tendencies in architectural and urban ideology today: namely, through communication. Texts from planning and not from architecture were selected since the theme to be dealt with, the street, has to do with urban configuration as it affects those instances we call public places. The texts chosen for examination are those by Richard Meier and Melvin Webber.[12] Different kinds of criteria guided this choice. The first was that of generality. These texts are general enough to include almost every theoretical problem. Second, these texts have had a considerable influence over the practice of design. They constitute the point of departure for a new form of architectural ideology. As such their influence may be seen on designers as varied in their approach as Cedric Price and Robert Venturi. Furthermore, they are related to the dominant ideology of the present stage of capitalism.

These texts try to relate several physical/formal aspects to certain functional aspects, emphasizing the latter through their communications approach.

One may argue that these texts get very close to the problem of signification but still fail to acknowledge it. They deal mainly with the problem of communication. Although these two areas, communication and signification, are tightly linked, the difference between the development of these respective discourses remains quite radical. It is therefore necessary to establish the essential nature of their interrelationship. Four constituent elements of the communications model appear in the various works of Meier and Webber, sometimes explicitly in Meier, sometimes implicitly in Webber. These elements are: sender, receiver, information, and channel.

In all these works two aspects of the model are consistently emphasized: (1) the channel, which allows for the transmission of information and (2) the quantity and distribution of information. The sender (that is, addresser) and receiver (that is, addressee) are mainly considered as the origin and destination of this information. The channel is seen by these authors as the basic element in the process of communication. The aspect emphasized in the communications process is the transportation of information. This paradigm successfully prevents these authors from inquiring into the nature of the information being communicated. Meier and Webber totally ignore the nature of the message or for that matter the language of which these messages are a part, as well as the structure of codes that make communication possible. In other words, even if the complete model is being used, there is no understanding of the positive theoretical implications of the notions of code and message and, therefore, little concern for the potential importance of these factors. This particular use of the communications model does not consider any aspects that are capable of rendering the communications model a theoretically positive concept. They ignore the potential of a complete model and particularly the role that message and code may play within a more complete model. The theoretical consequences of introducing the notions of message and code into an analysis of the built environment is a proposition that demands to be explored extensively and carefully.

If one focuses on the message instead of the channel, new dimensions are revealed. The notion of message emphasizes the fact that any communication implicates language—or, in more general terms, the use of some system of signs such as natural language, Morse code, traffic lights, and so on. When the built environment is conceived as a carrier of messages, every material object—its real appearance or its properties—becomes a sign; that is, in the process of communication it becomes something that designates something different from the designating thing. The fulfillment of this process requires the framework of a language to be accepted by both addresser and addressee, allowing the transmission of information about certain facts or thoughts or emotional states. In other words, in the process of communication, messages carried by the built environment are made according to the rules of the particular system of signs being used.

The analysis of the nature of this system of signs must be distinguished from their use in communication, since the latter, under the notions of channel and information, is the only aspect to be studied by the communication theories of the built environment. An analysis of the nature of a system of signs, or of a system of signification, must begin with the development of the most important element in the model, namely, the notion of code. An indirect way of expressing the need for the notion of code is to state that the sense is never an intrinsic property of the message. The realization that the information is never an exclusive property of that message indicates the need for the notion of code.[13] Information seen as the meaning of a message depends upon the possibility of being able to select from a repertory of other possible messages and combinations according to certain rules.

Why has this notion of code not been considered? Moreover, why has it been excluded from the communications theories of the built environment? In my opinion the answer to this question may be found in certain "ideological obstacles"[14] linked to the origins of these theories, which repress the acknowledgment of this notion of code.

If one examines the background of the communications theories of planning, one finds that the works I mention have a double origin. On the one hand they continue to develop problems that belong to the area of urbanism; in this respect they are linked to the problems of the design of the environment at an urban scale, based on previously established models in architecture and urban design. On the other hand, they introduce notions belonging to the social sciences, in particular to sociology and social psychology, as a means for solving functional problems or, in general, dealing with nonphysical aspects of the built environment. The tradition that is followed in this instance, as it is related to the design disciplines of architecture and urbanism, is integral to the notion of functionalism. This tendency may be characterized by an overwhelming concern for fitness between form and function. These are seen as terms in a direct causal relationship in that the form can be derived from a function. Furthermore, this is regarded as a universal process in that any form may be considered to be the result of a function and to be natural inasmuch as the architect's role is to search for the form that ideally fits the function. This ideology is represented in the beginnings of urbanism in the work of people as diverse in orientation as Ebenezer Howard, Soria y Mata, and Le Corbusier.[15]

Concerning the notions incorporated from the social sciences, these also belong to a tendency known as functionalism, characterized by an approach preoccupied with causation and universalism.[16] The conjunction of the functionalist approaches of both architecture and the social sciences is the achievement of certain urban planning theories.

Design has always been based on a form/function polarity, oscillating between the two poles at different moments in history, emphasizing first one extreme and then the other. Our advanced ideological theories still play within this oscillation. In the case of the communications approach, the emphasis on information and its distribution results in an emphasis of the nonphysical or functional aspects. What is of major interest at this juncture is the fact that this functionalist conception of the environment relates to the form/function distinction; the underlying structural base of architectural ideology is thus certainly present in the communications approach to the urban environment.

The form/function distinction, which determines the design categories on which the activity of architecture has always been based, prevents the built environment from being approached in its signifying functions in a systematic way, either theoretically or practically. The functionalist approach presupposes a natural linkage between function and form, the latter being determined by the former. This preconception obstructs the development of the notion of code, the very notion that allows the functional relationship to be understood as only one of the structural links that determine the signifying nature of the built environment. In other words, to apprehend function, a set of forms must have been submitted to some kind of codification. Furthermore, function, though the most obvious, is not the unique meaning signified by the built environment.

There are several other meanings that, like function, are not linked in a direct way to form but are defined by the structural relations existing among different forms within a given culture. The use of an incomplete communications model is related to an operation wherein the elements of the model contradictory to functionalist ideology—such as message and code—are deliberately eliminated. The notions of causal, dual, universal, and natural that define all relations between form and function in this ideology serve as an obstacle to the development of a more adequate theoretical base. The concepts of code and message allow one to establish not only what is being communicated but also the structure of that which is being communicated; they predicate those organized repertories from which we may select and combine the messages, thus making it possible to establish specific relations, other than the functional, between form and meaning.

In examining the Meier/Webber communications approach one encounters at once the problem of defining the object of knowledge or theoretical object. What in their case is the theoretical object? Meier and Webber use a theory of communication that describes the causal relations existing between formal and functional aspects as manifest in an overall analysis of urban structure. However, the urban structure taken as a global whole cannot be considered a theoretical object; it is insufficient for this. What is called urban structure and to a lesser degree what is called the city, irrespective of any communications models, appear to us as wide sociocultural phenomena, as a sort of total social fact. Paraphrasing de Saussure[17] one could say that one is free to analyze this environment from an economic point of view, from a sociological, a political, a psychological, and aesthetic, or even an exclusively technical point of view. It is the multidimensional character of this *structure* that indicates that it cannot be taken as a whole and be subjected to a rigorous and unitary study. Taken as a whole it can only be approached as a heteroclitous set of observations implying multiple and different points of view, a plurality of pertinences.

It happens because this structure is nothing but the pure essence of the real object city, the product of a typical empiricist approach. The reason that the definition of the theoretical object is not stated precisely lies in the empiricist approach of Meier and Webber, which is based on the description of reality. The structure in this approach is the description of communication as it appears in any urban center that is not productively developed because of ideological obstacles. The more advanced environmental design ideologies—of which the communications model is a prime example—proffer raw material for the production of a theory of production of signification in the built environment. In particular, the critical analysis of the ideological notion of function together with its subversion is an initial stage that allows for the development of a concept that opposes and yet encompasses function. In this sense the concept of code appears as a more adequate (theoretical) model for the description of the built environment. But the concept of code is not enough to consider the built environment in terms of signification.

The consideration of the built environment or any other system as a system of signification implies that the information conveyed must be seen in terms of the culture that produces these objects. The notion of communication and the abstraction of universality are closely related.

Conversely, the notion of signification has its origin in an approach where the different systems of signs are defined in relation to a given culture. The sense of these signs is defined by the relations that link them to other signs, both within the specific system to which they belong and within an overall cultural system.

This work can only be carried out within a particular culture, since any object will have a different signification in different cultural contexts. In order to understand a cultural system one has to understand the cultural laws by which signification is produced by each, or in each, of the cultural subsystems that comprise the various systems of signification. This concept introduces a new understanding of culture. "The historical data on culture may be reexamined from the angle of significative information, as well as from the view of it being a system of social codes which allows information to be externalized as appropriate signs for entry into the public domains of a society."[18]

Public places such as the street provide another segment of the material for the development of the theoretical object. Public places are those configurations where the complexity of a given culture is most densely manifested. It would be possible to characterize these places as lumps of specific articulations comprising various cultural and social codes. In order to describe and explain the structure of these lumps in its entire complexity, it is necessary to propose a specific model for analysis.

The object of study may be reformulated as the production of signification in the built environment through the articulation of various cultural codes within a culture and a mode of production.[19] I call this object *place*.

Signification I: Signification as Structure

The semiotic approach to the theory of the environment determines the need for incorporating theoretical instruments developed in areas distinct from architecture, mainly in linguistics. It is interesting to see that from a broad functional approach, still within the constraints of a communications model, it is possible to pass from a concern for communication to one for signification and to enter at once into the problem of culture and cultural codes in the built environment. At this point it is illuminating to evoke the model of the linguist Roman Jakobson that deals with the functions of the message.[20]

The linguistic model of the message as proposed by Jakobson is a concept that may be most strictly applied to oral messages or to speech. Only oral/verbal language offers precise indicators as to the predominance of each of the respective functions of this model. On the other hand, it is also true that this Jakobson model has had, and still has, a specific role in semiotics: namely, to make manifest the characteristic nature of any message. The procedure is to reveal the six basic functions or areas of signification that, according to their links with each of the necessary elements in each act of communication, are clearly distinguishable at a theoretical level.[21]

An understanding of these functions compels one to go back to the constitutive factors in any act of communication. The *addresser* sends a *message* to the *addressee*. To be operative the message requires a *context* referred to, that is, the "referent," seizable by the addressee. The next prerequisite is the existence of a *code* fully, or at least partially, common to both the addresser and addressee—or, in other words, to the encoder and decoder of the message. Finally there is the essential condition of *contact*: a physical channel and psychological connection between sender and receiver of the message, enabling both of them to enter and stay in communication. All these factors may be schematized as follows:

Context

Addresser　　Message　　Addressee

Contact

Code

Each of these six factors determines a different function in language. This would also be true for the built environment, considered as signification. Although the six basic aspects of language are always present, one always tends to be emphasized at the expense of the others, depending on the context. The resultant diversity arises not out of a monopoly by one of these functions but through a different hierarchical ordering of these functions.[22]

When the message is set toward the referent, an orientation toward the *content*, it is called the *referential* function. It is the denotative aspect in language and although it is the predominant element in many messages, the other functions always have to be considered. If one regards this function as the equivalent to the "functional" aspect in the built environment—where a natural linkage occurs between form and function—it will seem as if a denotative relationship had appeared similar to that which occurs in language.[23] The so-called *emotive* or expressive function, focused on the *addresser*, aims a direct expression of the addresser's attitude toward what he is speaking about.[24]

When the orientation is toward the *addressee*, it is called the conative function; examples of this in language are the vocative and imperative ("Go out!" "Sit down!"). There are messages that serve primarily to establish, prolong, or discontinue communication, to check whether the channel works ("Hello, do you hear me?" "Are you listening?"). This emphasis on the *contact* is called the *phatic* function. Formulas or dialogues generated only for the purpose of establishing communication are other typical examples of it.[25] When the message is focused on the code, it performs a *metalingual* function; sometimes the addresser and the addressee need to check whether they are using the same code ("I don't follow you, what do you mean?"; or in anticipation of such a question, "Do you know what I mean?").[26] Finally the set toward the *message* itself, for its own sake, is the *poetic* function of language.[27] The study of the poetic function extends beyond the limits of poetry. The scheme of the factors may then be complemented by a corresponding scheme of their functions:

		Referential	
Emotive	Poetic		Conative
	Phatic		
	Metalingual		

Let us see how this model works in architecture by taking the case of the street as an example. If we approach the street from the point of view of the Webber/Meier communications model, the function that is emphasized is the referential. The referential function manifests itself here as a communication in the form of a channel, the media element linking origin and destination. Message and code are excluded by this emphasis, since there is neither concern for signification nor for the structure of messages. In a simplistic manner the street is considered merely as a channel where communication is solely transportation. The overriding concern is for the channel and not for the contact as opposed to Jakobson's model, where channel is considered in relation to the transmission of the messages between addresser and addressee.

In the traditional approach each element of the environment relates to a referent. But the referent is only one of the factors of the communication model, and the referential function only one of the functions. If one considers the street as a complex message rather than simply as a channel, other elements emerge which emphasize different functions. In the street as a complex message the functions manifest themselves as follows. The *referential* function is the act of circulating, wherein the street and a path in an open field are the same. The meaning circulation is here transmitted by a physical element, the surface of the ground, the horizontal plane, which in both instances functions as signifier.[28] With this referential function, the conative function regulates and imposes a mode of circulation by means of a system determining both permission and prohibition.

These controlling rules are brought into being through elements such as: sidewalk-street, crossings, block interruptions, traffic lights, and signs. Simultaneously, the *emotive* function also appears through elements that refer to an authorship: for example, the Paris Metro entrances designed by Guimard or the Parisian street as a whole in the avenues of Haussmann. Alternatively, such a function may be mediated through buildings; the Guggenheim Museum in New York is an example where the presence of the individual architect is strong. A comparable function may also be provided through graphic elements such as billboards. Elements that serve the *conative* function, such as traffic signs and lights or other kinds of signs, also possess a *metalingual* function through which every element insures the comprehension of another, referring to its code. This metaelement may be of very different constituent types, from language to objects that speak about objects. Thus a traffic light, by indicating "wait" and "walk," informs us that we are on a corner and also how we are supposed to act regarding this element in terms of traffic codes. A sign of a restaurant has the function of making sure that we understand the object as a restaurant.

There is also a metalingual function, present by connotation, in the case of display windows. The *phatic* function is one of the most difficult to find in a pure state in nonverbal cases. A good example, however, would be the advertising billboard, which, in view of the competition, tries to make sure that above all else contact is established. This is sometimes achieved with very strong lights, which are the first thing that attracts attention, even before communication is established through content. Finally, the *poetic* function is present in each and all of the examples given for the other functions. For example, the traffic sign system realizes a poetic function by means of design and color. Needless to say the poetic function plays a major role in the advertising code. In general, graphic advertising covers the conative function by means of the poetic; one may also cite sidewalk designs like the Copacabana strip in Rio de Janeiro or, alternatively, certain tree rhythms as examples.

None of these functions appear to exist in isolation. The elements never have just one function. The six are always present, though in varying hierarchical order. The definition of the model itself shows us the possibilities and limitations of its use. It is the case of a simple, exhaustive, and sufficiently abstract system of classification in order to allow extension to nonlinguistic areas.

However, a classification of signifying dimensions is not a theory for the mechanism by which they are produced. Jakobson's communication model permits us to view the built environment as a complex message and thereby to subvert the ideological notion of a single function through the discovery that each message must be seen as a sheaf of functions. Each of these functions implies a particular area of signification or meaning. The final understanding of these areas of signification is possible only when we apply the concept of code, since each function or area of signification is determined by a particular set of codes.

Through the use of the Jakobson model as a critical tool, it is possible to recognize the purely conventional, codified character of the form/function couple as the product of an extraordinary ideological set, operating in the technical or aesthetic realm, or in a combination of both.[29] At the same time Jakobson's model reveals the need for the systematization of the complex of cultural codes that are determined by the multiple functions implicit in the architectural object. However helpful the Jakobson model may be, it is insufficient for the specific study of the codes themselves.

From the foregoing initial stage we see that it is at least possible to consider the built environment in terms of signification, the different areas of signification corresponding to the different functions of the message. The next question is: What are the "elements and relationships" that make signification possible, that enable the signifying functioning of the built environment to come into being?

The study of the codes allows one to understand the mechanisms by which matter acquires the capability of transmitting meaning by establishing relations between matter and those different significations that are inscribed on it, thereby giving a configuration sense within a given culture. The study of codes has many sides and there are basically two ways in which it can be approached. On one hand we may analyze the codes as static structures. These structures are to be understood as different sets of rules combined in a particular way, underlying the built environment. On the other hand, these structures of sense have not always existed and are by no means immutable. These structures are produced and transformed in a process that is called *production of signification*. This second kind of analysis, which constitutes a second stage, is our prime concern, but in order to realize it, it seems necessary to go through an analysis of structures, the first stage.[30]

Signification II

What have been described as stages are in fact not simply stages but two alternative options with which the semiotic project is confronted. The first option is to approach the built environment as systems of signification as structured by communication—that is, by the transmission and exchange of messages, which is done by the exchange of signs in a game both within the sign (signifiers and signifieds) and, mainly, between signs.

De Saussure affords us an economic metaphor that defines the sign through the notion of value:

For a sign (or an economic value) to exist—as its linguistic value—it must be possible, on the one hand, to exchange dissimilar things (work and wage) and, on the other, to compare similar things with each other. That is, one can exchange five dollars for bread or for soap or for cinema tickets, but one can also compare this five dollars with ten or fifty dollars, etc. In a similar way a 'word' can be 'exchanged' for an idea (that is for something dissimilar), but it can also be compared with other words (that is with something similar). In English the word mutton derives its value only from its coexistence with sheep; the meaning being truly fixed only at the end of this double determination: signification and value.[31]

In the past few years in which the "analysis of sense" has been developing very fast, the ideological limitations of this structural approach to signification based upon the circulation of signs has become clear.[32]

The second option is that of approaching signification according to the possibilities initiated by the Marxist critique of economy and the consequent emphasis on the notion of productive work or production. Marx analyzes "value" in the circulation of merchandise, as a crystallization of social labor; that is, as the production previous to the circulation. Through this he reveals concepts such as surplus value which owe their existence to this production. This concept is "invisible"—Ricardo did not see it. It is hidden by the effect of the production; that is, the circulation of merchandise. This analysis of production allows Marx to develop a criticism of a system based on the exchange and circulation of the product. A parallel criticism has only recently been developed in semiotics, analyzing the circulation of signs in an analysis comparable to that developed by Marx with respect to the circulation of money. "At the level of society, language functions as money, which allows the exchange of information but hides the production of sense."[33]

The whole dilemma facing architectural semiotics today seems to lie in the following area: either continue to formalize architecture as a semiotic system from the point of view of communication or else open, within the interior of the problem of communication (which inevitably constitutes the entire social problem), a whole other consideration, that which refers to the *production of sense previous to sense.* Referring to the current semiotic problem in literature, Kristeva states that ". . . it is effectively impossible to understand what such a semiology is speaking about when it formulates a problem of a production which is not equivalent to communication even if produced through it, if the breaking point which neatly separates the problematic of exchange from that of labor is not accepted."[34] In this field of analysis, a semiotic of the built environment, one has to develop and go through those two stages of exchange and production at the same time, since for architecture, unlike the field of literature, the first stage, a semiotic of the sign (in relation to communication), is virtually nonexistent. The brief analysis of the built environment considered as a sheaf of functions may be considered as one of the first steps toward a structural semiotic (or semiotic of the sign) in the built environment.

In the theoretical analysis I propose to develop, in the perspective of production (the second option), *signification is not thought of as what the "thing" communicates but as the readings that, within a given culture, may be produced out of it*—the readings that this culture allows. In this sense the street as one of the public places in our society appears as an extremely valuable material. It condenses, explains, reproduces the multiple sociocultural codes of our society. What we call culture is thought of as codes that organize different chains or systems, such as theater, gesture, politics, writing. These codes are no longer seen as the product of an analysis in front of the communicating object, as a classification and abstraction of an inventory that finds fixed and finite sets of regularities and rules. These codes are considered instead as forces in a dynamic process that both produces and transforms sense according to determined conditions of production.[35] The problem is then how to reveal these forces without reducing them to a system, to a closed construction.

From the problem of the codes as process one finds the need for analyzing an aspect that I believe is a priority. I am referring to the mode of articulating codes, which should be distinguished from the study of the codes themselves. If the study of the codes from the point of view of communication of meaning is based on the principle of unity, which allows one to recognize similarities and differences (value), what guides the work of reading is what could be called the principle of dispersion. This principle does not close a system, which is precisely what characterizes architecture and design, but opens it, allowing for an articulation of various readings as structured by the codes.[36] Each reading develops a series of chains at the signifier level, which slides over a mosaic of signifieds belonging to the same context. It is as if points of a network were being linked neither by chance nor in accordance with a preconceived plan. It is this process of "chaining" that constitutes the structuring force.

The polysemy or multiplication of significations produced by this plural reading, that is, by an articulation of the codes, does not act as an addition to the old fixed structure, which remains untouched, but rather makes us enter a new dynamic space, that of work and the production of sense. One may think of the articulation between readings as that which opens the system, which forces the movement of sense; as that which allows us to enter into the production of signification and permits us to think of a practice based on the work on such mechanisms and on the structuring conditions of signification in the built environment.

1968–1972

Notes

This article is based on the work, "La Structure Urbaine; Communication, Pratique, Apprentissage" (developed under a Fellowship from the French government at the Centre de Recherche d'Urbanisme, Paris, in 1967–68), in which I analyzed the street as a system of signification. Most of the original content has been preserved. However, some changes have been made in order to put it in the context of this book and to incorporate some of the hypotheses that are in continuing development from the earlier work. Consequently, some quotations have a later date.

1. Louis Althusser and Etienne Balibar, *Lire Le Capital* (Paris: Maspero, 1967), references from the English edition, *Reading the Capital* (London: NLB, 1970).

2. Developed in D. Agrest, "On the Ideology of Urban Planning," University of Buenos Aires, 1969, and in more detail in "Critical Remarks on Urban Planning Models," a lecture given at the Institute for Architecture and Urban Studies, New York, March 1972.

3. Althusser, *Lire Le Capital*, p. 36.

4. Ibid., p. 38.

5. Ibid.; this passage, translated from the Spanish language edition (Buenos Aires: Ed. Siglo XXI, 1969, p. 44), remains only as a paraphrase in the English edition.

6. Ibid., p. 41; Althusser continues: "When Marx tells us that the production process of knowledge . . . takes place entirely in knowledge, in the 'head' or in thought, he is not for one second falling into an idealism of consciousness, mind or thought, for the '*thought*' we are discussing here is not a faculty of a transcendental subject or absolute consciousness confronted by the real world as *matter*: . . . This thought is the historically constituted system of an *apparatus of thought*, founded on and articulated to natural and social reality."

7. Ibid., pp. 41–42.

8. L. Althusser, "Practica Teorica y Lucha Ideologica," published in a collection of articles, *La Filosofia como Arma de la Revolucion* (Cordoba: Ed. Pasado y Presente, 1968), p. 37.

9. Ideology is a set of representations and beliefs (religious, moral, political, aesthetic) that refer to nature, to society, and to the life and activities of men in relation to nature and society. Ideology has the social function of maintaining the global structure of society by inducing men to accept consciously the place and role assigned to them by this global structure. In this way, ideology gives a certain distorted knowledge of the world; "ideology in a way alludes to reality, but it only offers an illusion of this reality." Architectural ideology—an ideological subregion—then can be seen as the summation of Western architectural knowledge in its entire range, from commonplace intuition to sophisticated theories and histories of architecture. This ideology has explicitly claimed to serve the practical needs of society by ordering and controlling the built environment. Nevertheless, I hold that the underlying function of this ideology is the pragmatic one of serving and preserving the overall structure of society in Western social formations—that is, the capitalist model of production and architectural practice as a part of it. D. Agrest and M. Gandelsonas, "Semiotics and Architecture: Ideological Consumption or Theoretical Work," *Oppositions* I (1973), pp. 93–100.

10. Semiotics, the theory of systems of signs, is considered to be only a first stage toward a future general theory of ideologies. In this stage semiotics not only can provide models but it can also suggest theoretical strategies in our battle against a specific ideology, architectural ideology.

11. Concrete concepts "'realise' theoretical concepts in the concrete knowledge about concrete objects" in a dialectical process. ". . . it is possible to say that the concrete knowledge about a concrete object presents itself to us as the 'synthesis' Marx speaks about. A synthesis of the necessary theoretical concepts (in a strict sense) combined with the elaborated . . ." concrete concepts. L. Althusser, "Acerca del Trabajo Teorico" in *La Filosofia Como Arma de la Revolucion*.

12. Richard Meier, *A Communications Theory of Urban Growth* (Cambridge, Mass.: The MIT Press, 1962); Melvin Webber, "Order in Diversity; Community Without Propinquity," in L. Wingo, Jr., ed., *Cities and Space: The Future Use of Urban Land* (Baltimore: Johns Hopkins University Press, 1963), and "The Urban Place and the Non-Place Urban Realm," in Webber, ed., *Explorations into Urban Structure* (Philadelphia: University of Pennsylvania Press, 1964).

13. W. Ross Ashby, *An Introduction to Cybernetics* (London: Chapman and Hall, 1956).

14. I refer here to function and functionalism as major ideological obstacles that will be partly explored.

15. The relationship between the functionalism of these urbanists and the functionalism underlying the work of the planners I criticize (among others) has been developed in research on the ideology of urban planning where I investigated its origins. D. Agrest, "La Ideologia del Planeamiento Urbano" [The Ideology of Urban Planning] (Universidad de Buenos Aires, 1969).

16. I refer to the functionalism of Emile Durkheim and the structural functionalism of Talcott Parsons. For a criticism of functionalism see Claude Lévi-Strauss, "Functionalist Theories of Totemism," *Totemism* (Boston: Beacon Press, 1963); *Structural Anthropology* (New York: Basic Books, 1963).

17. Ferdinand de Saussure, *Course in General Linguistics* (New York: McGraw-Hill, 1966).

18. "The conception of culture as information determines certain methods of research. It authorizes in particular the analysis of cultural stages, as well as the set of historical and intellectual facts conceived as infinite texts; and it allows at the same time the use of methods of semiotics and structural linguistics." Jury M. Lotman, "Problèmes de la Typologie des Cultures," in *Essays in Semiotics* (The Hague: Mouton, 1971; my translation).

19. This will be part of a general theory that will study the nature of the functioning of ideological phenomena: in J. Kristeva's terms "a general theory of superstructure," the object of this theory being the social production of sense. Julia Kristeva, "La Semiologie comme science; Critique et/ou critique de la science," *La Nouvelle Critique* 16 (1968). Eliseo Veron, "Vers une logique naturelle des mondes sociaux," *Communications* 20 (1973), p. 247.

20. Roman Jakobson, "Linguistics and Poetics," closing statement in T. Sebeok, ed., *Style in Language* (Cambridge, Mass.: The MIT Press, 1960); page references, paperback edition, 1971.

21. Throughout this section I closely paraphrase Jakobson, "Linguistics," p. 354.

22. Ibid.

23. Diana Agrest and Mario Gandelsonas, "Critical Remarks on Semiology and Architecture," *Semiotica* IX (1972), pp. 252–271.

24. "The purely emotive stratum in language is presented by the interjections. . . . If we analyze language from the standpoint of the information it carries, we cannot restrict the notion of information to the cognitive aspect of language. A man, using expressive features to indicate his angry or ironic attitude, conveys ostensible information, and evidently this verbal behavior cannot be likened to such nonsemiotic, nutritive activities as 'eating grapefruit.'" Jakobson, "Linguistics," p. 354.

25. "'Well,' the young man said, 'well'" she said, 'well, here we are' he said, etc. The endeavor to start and sustain communication is typical of talking birds. It is also the first verbal function acquired by infants; they are prone to communicate before being able to send or receive informative communication." Ibid., p. 355.

26. The following dialogue is given by Jakobson as an example: "The sophomore was plucked."—"But what is plucked?"—"Plucked means the same as flunked."—"And flunked?" "To be flunked is to fail in an exam."—"And what is sophomore?" . . . "A sophomore is [or means] a second year student." Ibid., p. 356.

27. "The political slogan 'I like Ike', succinctly structured, consists of three monosyllables and counts three diphthongs/ay/each of them symmetrically followed by one consonantial phoneme, / . . . I . . . k . . .k/. The make up of three words presents a variation: no consonantial phonemes in the first word, two around the diphthong in the second, and one final consonant in the third." Ibid., p. 357. The secondary poetic function of this electional catch phrase reinforces its impressiveness and efficacy and covers the conative function. It is typical of advertising to cover the conative function with a poetic function.

28. I use "signifier" here, according to de Saussure, as one of the two sides of a sign. The sign is a two-sided linguistic unit that exists through the association of a sound image of *signifier* and a concept of *signified*. De Saussure, *Course in General Linguistics*.

29. Cf. D. Agrest, M. Gandelsonas, J. C. Indart, "On Semiotics, Perverse Objects and Ideological Texts" in *Summa* (Buenos Aires), no. 32 (1970); also, E. Veron, "Semiotics and the Social Production of Knowledge," in *Structuralism Around the World*, Thomas Sebeok, ed. (The Hague: Mouton).

30. Agrest and Gandelsonas, "Semiotics and Architecture."

31. De Saussure, *Course in General Linguistics*..

32. See criticism developed by J. Derrida, *De la Grammatologie* (Paris: Ed. de Minuit, 1967); Kristeva, "Semiologie comme science"; E. Veron, "Pour une Semiologie des opérations translinguistiques," *Versus* 4 (1972).

33. Derrida, *De la Grammatologie.*

34. Kristeva, "Semiologie comme science."

35. Roland Barthes, *S/Z* (Paris: Ed. du Seuil, 1970).

36. Ibid.

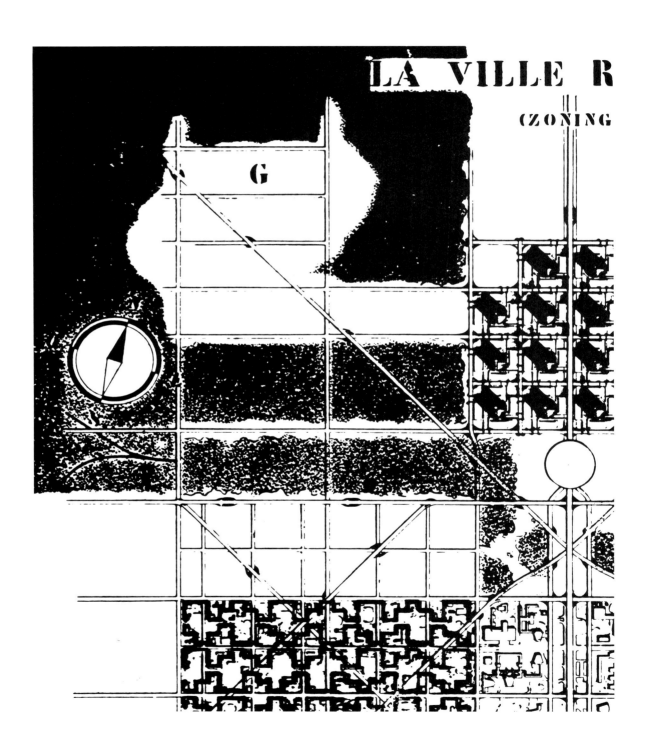

The specific relationship of architecture to ideology has been generally excluded from consideration in traditional architectural criticism. Concerned only to relate architecture formally, or internally, to itself, or at best to relate architecture externally to society in general, criticism has failed to truly incorporate the *cultural* problematic of architecture into its domain of concern. When the cultural dimension has been introduced, it has more often been as a simple explanation of architecture as "reflecting" a particular culture—the notion of style as the expression of the spirit of the age—than as a problem to be confronted independently from a consistent theoretical standpoint.

Practicing architects and critics of architecture have repeatedly emphasized the need to relate architecture to its social or cultural context. Positions have been developed around such concepts as "contextualism" and "ugly and ordinary" by writers like Colin Rowe and Denise Scott Brown and Robert Venturi. Rowe, for example, speaks of an architectural contextualism that situates the object of design or analysis in its physical-historical surroundings in terms of formal elements and relations; Venturi and Scott Brown speak of the need to recognize mass culture as *the* necessary cultural product of our time and as a new source of inspiration for designers. However, rather than attempting to appeal to the notion of collage—a familiar architectural strategy in periods of transition—or to the simulation of the objects of mass culture, this analysis will attempt to investigate the mechanisms of the built environment at this specific historical moment.

I wish to explore here these "external" or cultural relations of architecture—that is, between architecture and its social context—by means of a theoretical model that posits two distinct forms of cultural, or symbolic, production. The first, which I shall call *design*, is that mode by which architecture relates to cultural systems outside itself; it is a normative process and embraces not only architectural but also urban design. The second, which is more properly called *non-design*, describes the way in which different cultural systems interrelate and give form to the built world; it is not a direct product of any institutionalized design practice but rather the result of a general process of culture.

In thus examining the mechanisms which relate architecture to culture—the processes by which meaning is produced, not only within architecture or design, but also in the domain of non-design—we are, of course, analyzing ideology itself. For ideology is no more than the social production of meaning. Thus, all cultural production, such as architecture, when articulated at the economic and political levels, manifests the ways by which ideology is produced as a part of a given social structure.[1]

In this sense, it is unnecessary to compare one type of architecture to any other type of architecture—as in the accepted mode of "formal," internal criticism—or to compare it to society in general. Rather, one must oppose the notion of architecture as *design* to the notion of a radically different kind of symbolic configuration—*non-design*. This opposition allows analysis of the built environment in terms of the relationship between different cultural systems. Design and non-design, in fact, can be seen as two modes of social discourse; and to consider them in this way opens up the question of what might be called the "active relationship" between design, as one cultural system, and other cultural systems.

Design and Culture

Design, considered as both a practice and a product, is in effect a closed system—not only in relation to culture as a whole, but also in relation to other cultural systems such as literature, film, painting, philosophy, physics, geometry, etc. Properly defined, it is reductive, condensing and crystallizing general cultural notions within its own distinct parameters. Within the limits of this system, however, design constitutes a set of practices—architecture, urban design, and industrial design—unified with respect to certain normative theories. That is, it possesses specific characteristics that distinguish it from all other cultural practices and that establish a boundary between what is design and what is not. This boundary produces a kind of *closure* that acts to preserve and separate the ideological identity of design. This closure, however, does not preclude a certain level of permeability toward other cultural systems—a permeability which nevertheless is controlled and regulated in a precise way.

Culture, on the other hand, is understood to be a system of *social codes* that permit information to enter the public domain by means of appropriate signs. As a whole, culture can be seen as a hierarchy of these codes, manifested through various texts.[2]

The relationship between design and culture may, then, be stated as the mode by which design is articulated (as one cultural system) in relation to other cultural systems (at the level of codes). The transformations in these articulations are historically determined, and they display themselves as changes in the structures of meaning. Thus, the development of specific forms of articulation between design and other cultural systems can be seen as a dynamic process, the study of which opens up the problem of the production of meaning.

The relationship between design and other cultural systems is heightened and intensified at certain moments in this process, and its precise articulations become clearer. In architecture, this occurs when new economic, technical, functional, or symbolic problems force the production of new formal repertories, or the expansion and transformation of existing vocabularies.

Thus, during the French Enlightenment, elementary geometrical figures (the sphere, the pyramid, the cube, etc.) were introduced as the primary constituents of a new formal vocabulary by the "revolutionary" architects Boullée and Ledoux. For Ledoux these forms expressed the new notions of the *sublime*, while for Boullée they represented the universe and its scientific explanation developed in the context of profound social and political change.[3]

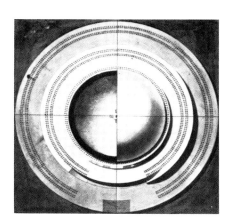

Plan of Newton's cenotaph. Etienne Boullée, 1784. Ink and wash.

Exterior by day.

Cross-section, interior night effect.

Cross-section, interior day effect.

Specificity

This recognition of articulations between design and other cultural systems also implies the recognition of differences between them—differences which may be understood through the notion of *specificity*.[4] This is a notion which permits the clarification of codes according to their relation to design or to other cultural systems.

Three types of codes regulate the interpretation and production of texts in design. First, there are those codes which may be seen as exclusive to design, such as codes establishing relationships between plans and elevations or plans and cross-sections. Second, there are those codes which are shared by various cultural systems, among which design is included (i.e., spatial, iconic). Third, there are those which, while they are crucial to one cultural system (such as rhythm to music), participate—albeit transformed—in another (such as architecture) by virtue of a shared characteristic, i.e., in the case of rhythm, the temporality of the sequence, audial in one case and visual in the other.[5] In a decreasing order of specificity, the first type of codes are specific to design, the second have a multiple specificity, and the third are non-specific.

The specificity of a signifying system is not, however, defined solely by the specificity of its codes, but also by the form in which those codes are articulated; that is to say, the combination of codes may be specific, although the codes themselves may or may not be specific to the system in question.[6] Examples of specific code articulation in architecture are found in classical theories of harmony that utilize the articulation of musical codes and arithmetical proportional series for the invention of specific *architectural* codes, which are then used to determine the proportions of and relationships between the different elements of a building.

Specificity manages to maintain the limits of architecture despite the apparent changes that occur under the pressures of history, technology, social action, or symbolic change. On the one hand, the most specific codes remain within the system of architecture; on the other hand, the less specific codes link design with other systems through the opening and closing of its limits. This mechanism allows for the articulation of design with some systems and not with others, a process which operates according to the "internal" determinations of design—that is,

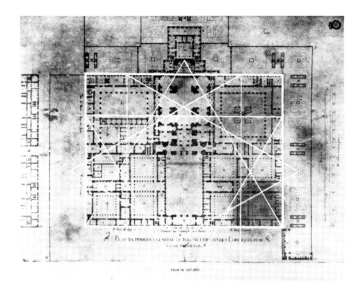

The Quadro of the Escorial in relation to Vitruvius's astrological plan (René Taylor).

The cosmological man superimposed on the plan of the Escorial (René Taylor).

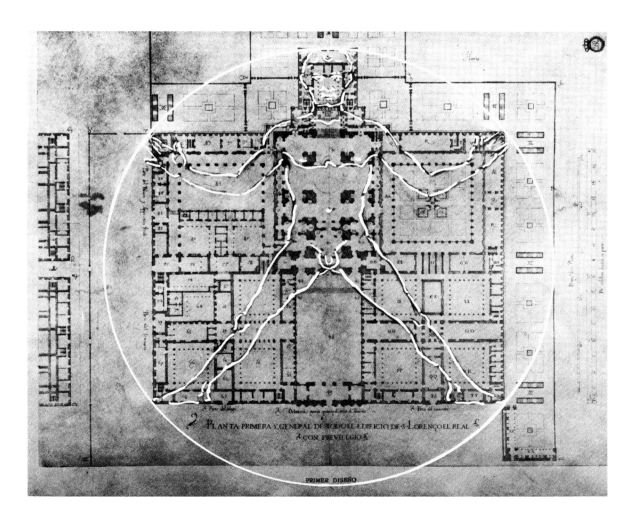

according to the rules of architectural language, to the logic of the configuration, and to the meaning proper of the "text" of design.[7]

The Mannerist inversion of the established architectural rules—by which each element is used in contradiction to what should be its prevailing ideological function—is an excellent example of such internal determination, in which the inversions so weaken the limits of architecture as to allow an opening to codes external to it; thus the "painterly" architecture of the sixteenth century in Italy.[8]

This process of articulation might, however, take place according to "external" determinations—to the forces of economics, politics, or other ideologies foreign to design. The influence of hermetic thought on the design of the Escorial Palace, for example, demonstrates the role of such external factors in architecture. Both the plan and the general configuration seem to have been derived from mystical or hermetic geometric regulating lines, based partly on parallel developments in quantitative mathematics, and partly on chapters eliminated from Renaissance editions of Vitruvius,[9] but not, as might be assumed, directly from classical architectural theory. Magic codes were thus substitutes for the Albertian geometric codes. Geometry, while represented by similar figures, was imbued with an entirely different meaning. At the same time, these geometric magic codes remained distinctly separate from other magic codes, such as those based on verbal or gestural practices which never entered in their physical-spatial implications into architecture.

Metaphoric Operations in Design

The concept of the closing and opening of limits introduces the notion of an ideological *filtering* in the production of design, which takes place by means of certain processes of symbolization. In this case an equivalence, or exchange, of sense is produced by restricting the access of certain codes and figures from other systems into architecture.

The notions of *metaphor* and *metonymy* allow for a more systematic analysis of this symbolic functioning. These should be considered as the mechanisms of opening and closure, ultimately revealing the way in which design maintains its limits in relation to culture and acts as a filter in relation to meaning.[10]

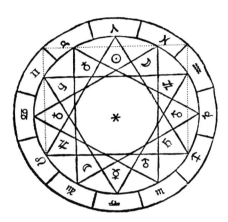

Astrological configuration (Julius Firmicus Maternus).

The liner Flandre. *Le Corbusier.*

The liner France. *Le Corbusier.*

Metaphor and metonymy are, of course, notions that have been used principally in the analysis of discourse and text. Since in this context we are analyzing the *production* of meaning and not its structure, the reference in general will be to metaphoric or metonymic *operations* rather than to these figures as they are applied to classical rhetoric.[11]

These tropes or rhetorical figures represent the most condensed expression of two basic kinds of relationship in discourse: the relation of similarity, which underlies the metaphor, and the relation of contiguity, which determines the metonymy. Each may exist in the relationship between the figure and the content or in the relation between figure and figure.

The development of any discourse (not necessarily a spoken one, and in this case the architectural discourse) may develop along two semantic-syntactic lines; one theme in the expression or content may lead to another either by means of similarity or by means of contiguity.[12] The most appropriate term for the former relation is "metaphoric" while the latter might be termed "metonymic."[13]

In its relationship to other cultural systems, which is a necessary condition for the regeneration of sense, architecture takes part in a game of substitutions which, thought of in terms of metaphoric or metonymic operations, explains, at the most specific level of form, the translation from extra-architectural to intra-architectural systems in a recoding which, by means of reducing meanings, maintains the limits of architecture.

The well-known nautical metaphor in Le Corbusier's Villa Savoye exemplifies this functioning. Here, two different signifying systems are related: dwelling and ocean liner. The necessary condition for this relationship is provided by the existence of an element common to both, in this case the window. Through a metaphoric operation, a figurative substitution of the signifying element common to both systems is produced (dwelling/window—liner/window), carrying and transferring codes from one system (liner) to the other (house). The new form is thus loaded with the new meanings required to translate into figures the proposed new architectural ideology.

The liner Aquitania. *Le Corbusier.*

The deck of the Aquitania. *Le Corbusier.*

The operation involved may be explained by the following propositions:

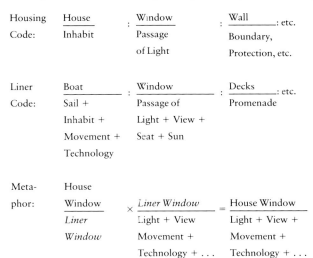

| Housing Code: | $\dfrac{\text{House}}{\text{Inhabit}}$ | : | $\dfrac{\text{Window}}{\text{Passage of Light}}$ | : | $\dfrac{\text{Wall}}{\text{Boundary, Protection, etc.}}$: etc. |

| Liner Code: | $\dfrac{\text{Boat}}{\text{Sail + Inhabit + Movement + Technology}}$ | : | $\dfrac{\text{Window}}{\text{Passage of Light + View + Seat + Sun}}$ | : | $\dfrac{\text{Decks}}{\text{Promenade}}$: etc. |

| Meta-phor: | $\dfrac{\text{House Window}}{\text{Liner Window}}$ | $\times$ | $\dfrac{\textit{Liner Window}}{\text{Light + View Movement + Technology} + \ldots}$ | $=$ | $\dfrac{\text{House Window}}{\text{Light + View + Movement + Technology} + \ldots}$ |

The similarity of functions—in this case, both liner and house are forms of habitation—makes the metaphor possible.

To these metaphoric transpositions other metonymic operations are added—for example, the *promenade architecturale*—which also carry further meanings related to the liner.

Functionalist Metaphors

At an urban scale, where the system of architectural design co-exists with many others almost by definition, the role of the metaphor as a filtering device becomes particularly evident, especially in the functional approach to urban design.

At the moment when urbanism was constituted as an institutionalized practice in the first decade of this century, urban formal codes were developed on the basis of the prevailing architectural codification. From the set of possible systems that give meaning to form, the functional approach was emphasized almost exclusively. Le Corbusier may serve once more to exemplify the type of functionalism that is at work in a filtering operation in the substitutive relation between architecture and other systems.

In Le Corbusier's texts *Vers une Architecture* (1923) and *Urbanisme* (1925), these metaphoric operations function clearly as a mechanism for contact between different cultural systems and, on other levels, as a means to architectural recodification.[14]

At the building scale, Le Corbusier establishes a connection between architectural systems and other systems, such as technology, tourism, sports, and geometry. This connection is established through a metaphor based on similarity of function.[15]

Geometry, for example, had acted as an internal code for formal control from the classical period of Greek architecture. It had not, however, functioned as the provider of the formal vocabulary itself, geometric regulating lines being the "invisible" elements in the construction. For Le Corbusier, however, geometry became not only an instrument of formal control, but also the provider of the formal vocabulary itself in two and three dimensions. The instrument (tool) for representation, that is, drawing, became first the project itself, and then the construction, without alteration.

At the urban scale, Le Corbusier's metaphoric operation establishes a relation between geometry as a signifying system and the city by means of the common element of "order," which is manifested as a "grid"; a system of equivalences is established between the geometric grid with its connoted codes and the city grid with the set of values ascribed to it by Le Corbusier.

Thus, in *Urbanisme*, the existing city is seen as equivalent to disorder, chaos, illness, and irrationality. On the other hand, the grid, the geometric order, is seen as equivalent to order, health, beauty, reason, modernity, and progress. "Geometry is the foundation. . . . It is also the material basis on which we build those symbols which represent to us perfection and the divine. . . ."[16]

In the plans for the Ville Contemporaine, and later for the Ville Radieuse, Le Corbusier establishes the equivalence between those two systems by means of the common element of grid-order. The appropriate connoted codes of the geometric grid are transferred through a figurative substitution to the city plan and become the codes of the city itself.

Satellite cities, e.g.,
government buildings or
center for social studies,
etc.

The business center

Railroad station and air
terminal

Hotels
Embassies

Housing

Factories

Warehouses

Heavy industry

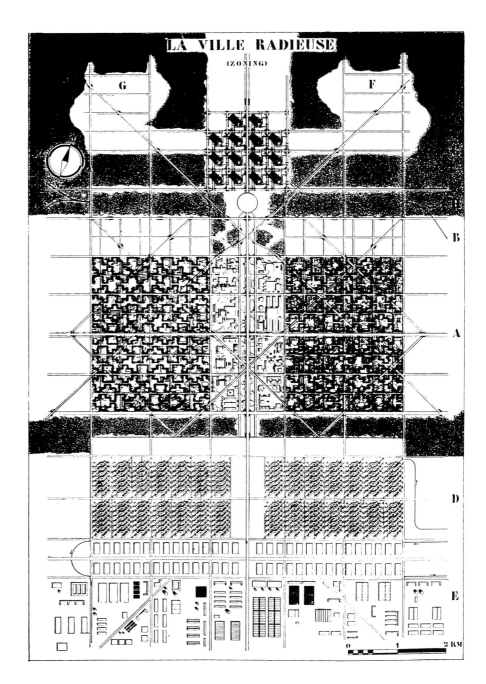

The Radiant City. Le Corbusier, architect,
1933. Zoning diagram.

It can be seen, in this case, that while there is an initial opening of the system, its closure is produced by means of a metaphorical equivalence by which the means of representation are imposed as ideological filters in order to develop an architectural recodification. In this substitution, meanings are limited and filtered by a system (geometry) which, while it may not be specific to architecture, will, in its recoding, become specific to urban design. This is made possible by the fact that a system such as geometry may participate in a double "game": symbolic at a formal-cultural level, and instrumental, or representative, at the level of the specific practice where physical configuration becomes the device that allows for translation and recoding.

The relationship between geometry as a symbolic system on the one hand, and as a basic organizational system on the other, is not, of course, a new problem and may be found at other points in the history of architecture. In the work of Piranesi, for example, the figurative and the geometric coexist, juxtaposed in a clear dialectical relationship. The rear of the altar of S. Maria del Priorato, for example, crudely displays the set of geometric volumes which serve as its support, while the face

Diagram implying the expansion of organic networks.

Network of street elevations.

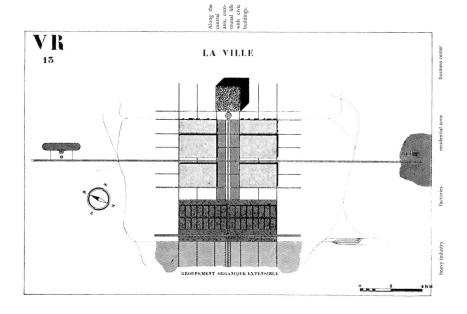

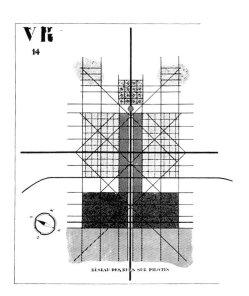

Study for the alter of S. Basilio in S. Maria del Priorato, Rome. G. B. Piranesi, c. 1764.

presents itself as almost pure allegory. The architectural contradiction between geometry and symbolism is here critically posed.[17]

When Boullée and Ledoux adopted geometry in itself as a formal system, the sacred symbology was substituted for a more secular symbology—that of man. In Le Corbusier, however, there is no longer a separation between the geometric and the symbolic; rather geometry itself represents the symbolic aspect of form, and carries with it an entire set of implicit values.

The Critique of Functionalism

With the waning of the enthusiasm for functionalism in the late 1940s, a series of works appeared which, conscious of the cultural reductivism of the heroic period, were explicitly concerned with the cultural rather than the functional aspects of design. This cultural concern was demonstrated by an intention to make explicit the articulation between architecture and other cultural systems.[18] The work of the active members of Team 10 (Alison and Peter Smithson) reintroduces culture in this sense, and again new openings and closures are produced by means of metaphoric operations: openings to incorporate "the culture"; closures to preserve the specificity of the system.

However, while in Le Corbusier the metaphor was reductive in terms of the possible inclusion of other cultural systems—a product of the exclusive nature of geometry and its concomitant modernism—the intention of Team 10 was to establish relations between architecture and other systems. "Our hierarchy of associations," they stated, "is woven into a modulated continuum representing the true complexity of human associations. . . . *We must evolve an architecture from the fabric of life itself*, an equivalent of the complexity of our way of thought, of our passion for the natural world and our belief in the ability of man."[19]

This criticism addresses itself precisely to the functionalist reductivism of the 1920s and to its elimination of cultural aspects, here described as "human associations" and "the fabric of life itself." These aspects were considered as an intrinsic aspect of architecture by Team 10.

Once more, metaphor is being used as the substitutive operation to incorporate "vital" aspects into design. Two types of metaphor are used. The one, which accounts for urban form in general, resembles Le Corbusier's use of geometry at an urban scale. The other, which accounts for the realization of ideas at a building scale, is itself conceived as a fundamental element of urban design.

The first metaphoric operation links two systems through the common element "life," and thus relates the city to nature (a tree). Hence the plans for Golden Lane. The city is overlaid with the attributes of a tree and given qualities of growth, organicity, movement; at the level of form, the city is understood *as* a tree possessing a stem, branches, and leaves.

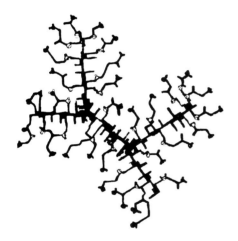

"Stem" development, Caen Herouville. Shadrach Woods, architect, 1961. Linear organization of activities and the proposed grouping of cells around the linear center.

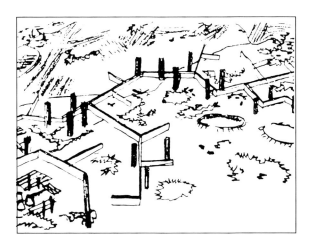

*Study for Golden Lane, London. Alison and
Peter Smithson, architects, 1952. Street deck
complex. The street mesh slots into the
vertical circulation of such complexes.*

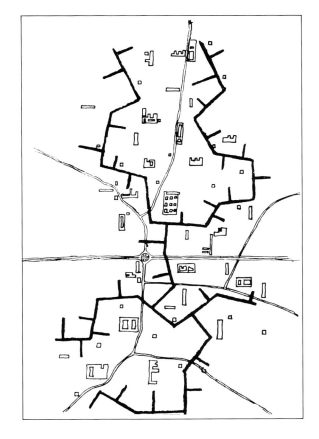

*"Urban re-identification," first diagram.
Peter Smithson, 1952.*

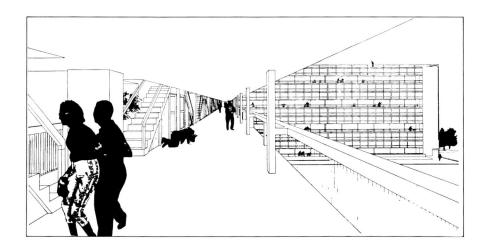

*Street equivalents, deck, housing. Peter
Smithson, 1953.*

$$\frac{\text{city/life}}{\textit{tree/life}} = \frac{\textit{tree/life}}{\text{branches, leaves, etc.}}$$

The second type of metaphoric operation articulates the relationship between design and life at the scale of the building and operates on the basis of a common function: circulation of people (street). In the proposal for Sheffield, the corridor is transformed through substitution into a street, carrying with it the urban codes which, when transferred to the building, give it "life."

Despite the explicit intent of Team 10 to open the system of architecture to culture, however, the result does not, in the end, differ much from the reductive system they criticize. The type of substitution utilized—the recodification of architecture by means of yet another formal analogy—is fundamentally similar to that effected by Le Corbusier. The process by which the Smithsons assimilate "life" to design is described exclusively in socio-cultural terms, even though "nature" is invoked, while the form adopted is taken directly from nature, that is, from organic, physical life. The other systems to which architecture is supposed to be actively linked (in this case, life or nature) are, in this way, filtered and reduced through the metaphor of one system, that of architectural forms. Thus, there is little real difference between the street in the air and the open corridor; the symbolic functioning which would make an architecture "out of life itself" is in fact absent. We may now see that metaphoric operations, rather than functioning to open the design system beyond its limits, in fact operate as filtering mechanisms which precisely define those limits.

It is paradoxical that the metaphor which allows for the interrelation of different codes is here used as a closing mechanism. Design is once again a sieve which allows the passage of certain meanings and not others, while the metaphor, which is used as a translating device from other codes to architecture, provides a mechanism by which ideology operates through design. In the infinite field of signifying possibilities, the metaphor defines, by a complex process of selection, the field of "the possible," thus consolidating itself in different regions by means of a language or languages.

Design/Non-Design

There is, however, another possible way of stating the relationship between design and culture. Rather than seeing systems of culture from a point of view that imposes a hierarchical relationship in which architecture or design is dominant, we may posit a notion of the "non-designed" built environment—"social texts," as it were, produced by a given culture.

The act of placing design (that is, both architecture and urban design) in relation to the rest of the built environment—the non-designed environment—immediately changes the level at which the problem is formulated. While in the work of Team 10 the problem is stated as internal to a single cultural system (architecture or urban design)—the relating of architecture to the city in such a way that the former acquires the "life" of the latter, here the signifying function of design is considered to relate to and, in relating, to oppose the rest of the built environment. It is regarded as a problem *internal to culture*, and thus to an entire set of cultural systems.

In these terms, architecture is no longer either implicitly or explicitly seen as the dominant system, but simply *one* of many cultural systems, each of which, including architecture, may be closed or "designed." But it is the entire set of different cultural systems configurating the built environment, which we call non-design.

In the world of non-design, that no-man's-land of the symbolic, and the scene of social struggle, internal analysis of single systems is revealed as inadequate and impossible to apply. Here there is no unique producer, no subject, nor is there an established rhetorical system within a defined institutional framework. Instead there is a complex system of intertextual relationships.

The opposition between design and non-design is fundamentally defined by three questions: first, the problem of *institutionality*; second, the problem of *limits and specificity*; and third, the problem of the *subject*. While the first establishes the relationship between design and non-design, the second establishes their respective types of articulation within culture (ideology), and the third establishes the processes of symbolization.

Design may be defined as a social practice that functions by a set of socially sanc-

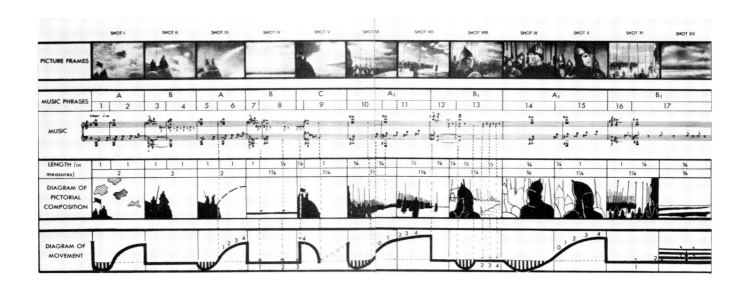

tioned rules and norms—whether implicit or explicit—and therefore is constituted as an institution. Its institutional character is manifested in the normative writings and written texts of architecture, which fix its meaning and, therefore, its reading. These texts insure the recording of the codes of design and guarantee their performance as filters and preservers of unity. They assure the homogeneity and closure of the system and of the ideological role it plays. The absence of a normative written discourse in non-design, on the other hand, precludes defining it as an institution and makes possible the inscription of sense in a free and highly undetermined way; we are here presented with an aleatory play of meaning. Thus, while design maintains its limits and its specificity, these defining aspects are lost in the semiotically heterogeneous text of non-design.[20]

Non-design is the articulation—as an explicit form—between different cultural systems. This phenomenon may be approached in two ways: as empirical fact— the actual existence of such systems found, for example, in the street, where architecture, painting, music, gestures, advertising, etc. coexist—and as a set of related codes. In the first instance, at the level of "texts," each system remains closed in itself, presenting juxtaposed manifestations rather than their relationships. At the level of codes, on the other hand, it is possible to discern the mode of articulation between the various systems and, in this way, to define the cultural and ideological overdetermination of the built environment, or rather the process by which culture is woven into it.[21] The predisposition of non-design to openness implies permeable limits and an always fluctuating or changing specificity.

Finally, if design is the production of an historically determined individual subject, which marks the work, non-design is the product of a social subject, the same subject which produces ideology. It manifests itself in the delirious, the carnivalesque, the oneiric, which are by and large excluded or repressed in design.

To study the reality of non-design and its symbolic production in relation to culture, it is necessary to perform an operation of "cutting"—"cutting" and not "deciphering," for while deciphering operates on "secret" marks and the possibility for discovering their *full* depth of meaning, cutting operates on a space of interrelations,[22] *empty* of meaning, in which codes substitute, exchange, replace, and represent each other, and in which history is seen as the form of a particular mode of symbolizing, determined by the double value of use and exchange of objects, and as a symbolic *modus operandi* which may be understood within that same logic of symbolic production and which is performed by the same social subject of ideology and the unconscious.[23]

The moment one object may be substituted for another beyond its "functional" use-value, it has a value added to it which is the value of exchange, and this value is nothing but symbolic. Our world of symbolic performances is comprised of a chain of such exchanges in meaning; that is how we operate within the realm of ideology. Non-design leaves this ideology in a "free-state," while design hides it.

The mode of analysis for these two phenomena of design and non-design (at least from the first moment that the difference between them is recognized) must therefore vary.

Reading. Mise-en-Séquence

As a complex social text, a semiotically heterogeneous object in which many different signifying matters and codes intervene, non-design has a disposition to be open to a situation which we will call here a *mise-en-séquence*.

We propose here for non-design a productive reading, not as the re-production of a unique or final sense, but as a way of retracing the mechanisms by which that sense was produced.[24] Productive reading corresponds to the expansive potential of non-design and permits access to the functioning of meaning as an intersection of codes. The object of analysis is not the "content," but the conditions of a con-

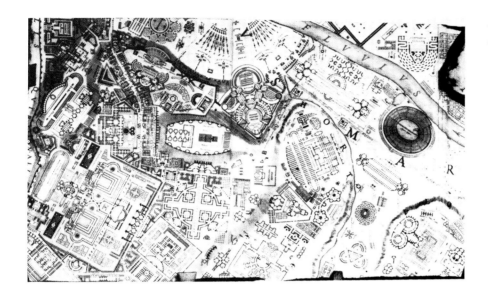

Plans for the Campo Marzio, Rome.

G. B. Piranesi.

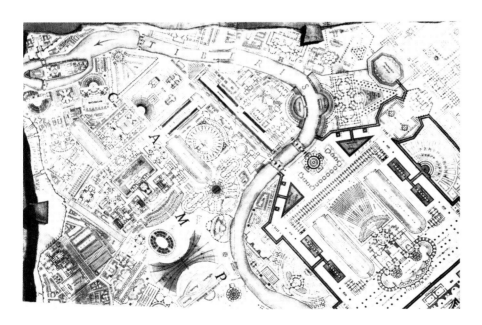

tent, not the "full" sense of design but, on the contrary, the "empty" sense which informs all works.[25] Instead of reading by following a previously written text, the reading starts from a "signifier of departure," not only toward an architectural text but toward other texts in culture, putting into play a force analogous to that of the unconscious, which also has the capacity to traverse and articulate different codes.

The metaphoric operation participates asymmetrically in both readings, design and non-design. While in design the metaphor is not only the point of departure but also the final point of the reading, in non-design the metaphoric and metonymic operations function similarly to dreams, as chains which permit access to meanings that have been repressed, thus acting as expansive forces. This expansive mechanism may be seen to be a device used for the purpose of criticism in the work of Piranesi. His opposition to the typological obsession of his time is an indication of his perception of the crisis of architecture and the consequent need for change and transformation. His Campo Marzio is a true architectural "explosion" that anticipates the destiny of our Western cities.[26] Piranesi's "explosive" vision comprises not just the architectural system per se but rather a system of relationships, of contiguity and substitution.

Non-design may also be seen as an explosive transformation of design. This kind of explosion implies in some way the dissolution of the limits of architecture, of the ideological limits which enclose different architectural practices.

In front of two drawings of Piranesi's Carceri, one of the Carcere Oscura of 1743 from the series of the Opere Varie and the other on the Carceri Oscure from the Invenzioni, the Russian filmmaker Eisenstein makes a reading which may be considered as an example of this type of analysis. Eisenstein applies a cinematographic reading to the first prison, his reading producing displacements with respect to the limits imposed by pictorial and architectural codes, thereby making it "explode" in a kind of cinematographic sequence.[27] This is the starting point of a reading that travels across literary, political, musical, and historical codes, multiplying in this way perceptions which are potential in the Piranesian work. A proof of this potential lies in Eisenstein's reading of Piranesi's second engraving, done eighteen years later, in which Eisenstein finds that the second is actually an explo-

Dark Prison. *G. B. Piranesi, 1743.*
Engraving.

Sergei Eisenstein's schematic sketch of
Piranesi's Dark Prison.

Prison of the Invenzioni. *G. B. Piranesi,*
1761. Engraving.

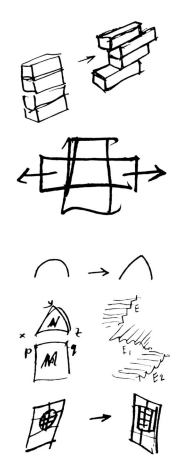

Sergei Eisenstein's sketches for his analysis of Piranesi's Dark Prison.

sion of the first prison, done by Piranesi himself.[28] It should be noted that Eisenstein is here dealing with a closed cultural system, such as architecture or painting. What Eisenstein takes, however, is not just *any* closed work from these fields but rather the work of someone like Piranesi, who poses the problem of the explosion in form (or form as explosion) in his Carceri, or in his Campo Marzio, which is a delirium of typological chaining. Although this Piranesian strategy touches problems specific to architecture, it also comes very close to the problem of the explosion of sense in architecture, to the problem of meaning as signifying chaining. In creating this extreme situation, Piranesi is implicitly assessing the problem of the limits of architecture as a "language," that is, as a closed system.

Fragments of Reading

One evening, half asleep on a banquette in a bar, just for fun I tried to enumerate all the languages within earshot: music, conversations, the sounds of chairs, glasses, a whole stereophony of which a square in Tangiers (as described by Severo Sarduy) is the exemplary site. That too spoke within me, and this so-called 'interior' speech was very like the noise of the square, like that amassing of minor voices coming to me from the outside: I myself was a public square, a sook; *through me passed words, tiny syntagms, bits of formulae, and no sentence formed, as though that were the law of such a language. This speech, at once very cultural and very savage, was above all lexical, sporadic; it set up in me, through its apparent flow, a definitive discontinuity: this* non-sentence *was in no way something that could not have acceded to the sentence, that might have been before the sentence; it was: what is eternally, splendidly, outside the sentence.*[29]

The built environment as the object of reading is not "seen" as a closed, simple unity but as a set of *fragments*, or "units of readings." Each of these units may be replaced by others; each part may be taken for the whole. The dimension of the built environment, empirically determined, depends upon the density of meanings, the "semantic volume."

Since these fragments appear as an articulation of different texts belonging to various cultural systems—e.g., film, art, literature—it is possible to read them by starting from any of these systems, and not necessarily from design.

Certain types of configurations, like public places (streets, plazas, cafes, airports), are ideal "fragments of readings," not only for their "semantic volume," but also for the complexity they reveal as to the signifying mechanisms in non-design. They may be characterized as signifying "nodes," where multiple codes and physical matter are articulated, where design and non-design overlap, and where history and the present are juxtaposed.[30]

The reading that can be produced by these places is not a linear discourse but an infinite and spatialized text in which those levels of reading, organized along various codes, such as theater, film, fashion, politics, gesture, are combined and articulated. The reading example we choose to present below is in itself metaphorical. It is the metaphor of architecture as theater. It is not a specific detailed analysis, but rather it exemplifies the mechanisms of chains and shifters.

Chains:

A metaphor begins to function by articulating the referential codes in relation to other codes by means of replacing the referential codes in the signifier of departure with another code. In this way, a chain linking the codes is developed. Once the intersemiotic metaphor, such as that between architecture and theater, is produced and a possible level of reading is established, the chain of signifiers along the codes and subcodes of that cultural system is organized by "natural association"—that is metonymically.

Signifiers appear and disappear, sliding through other texts in a play that moves along the codes of, for instance, the theater (i.e., scenic, gestural, decorative, acting, textual, verbal, etc.) in an intertextual network. This play continues until some signifier becomes another departure signifier, opening the network toward new chains through what we have called the *mise-en-séquence*, thus starting other readings from other cultural systems like film, fashion, etc. These signifiers which open to other systems may be called *shifters*.[31]

Shifters:

Such a reading presents a symbolic structure of a "decondensed" kind. Here, by decondensation we refer to an operation which is the reverse of that in the elaboration of dreams. Condensation and displacement are the two basic operations in

In front of the scene or in the scene

Theater

the pleasure of the gaze

decomposition

Cafe-Market

Cafe-Square

Cafe-Street

the word, any street is a scene

against the unity of representation

the scenic gesture

stage-costume-sex-transvestism

composition

. . .

multiplication of the gesture

objects as actors

facades as masks

actors as objects

mask-costume-ritual

space of action

space of spectacle

people as spectacle, politics

motion

and change

tension and center

unfolding of images in time

the narrative

light and montage

the unexpected, the gag

points of view and suspense

and transformation of the object

between fiction and reality

scale inversions

a space of sense

. . .

the eye of culture

the work of elaboration of dreams. By them, the passage is produced from the latent level to the manifest level of the dream. These two operations of condensation and displacement are two ways of displacing meanings, or of overdetermining, or giving more than one meaning to, some elements; they are produced precisely by means of the two operations already discussed, namely metaphor and metonymy. The metaphor corresponds to condensation, and metonymy to displacement.[32] In this way, it is possible to see the relationship between ideology (cultural codes) and subject (of ideology and of the unconscious) in the logic of symbolic production in the environment as determined by a particular mode of production.

Some signifier fragments function as "condensers" from which decondensation is possible through a network of meanings. These will be called "shifters." A set of readings could be regarded as a musical staff in which various signifiers are situated in a polyphonic organization with each voice at a different level of reading. Certain of these signifiers organize several different readings and allow for the intercrossing of codes and for the shifting from one to the next. These are the shifters; they are part of a process of exchange of codes. They are the conditions of the probability of producing different readings; they are structures of transition, the organizers of symbolic space. These connective, condensing structures are the key to the understanding of the complexity of the built environment as an infinite text. They are not concerned with signification but with the linking of signifiers. They are the key to an intertext where meanings are displaced, thereby forming a network in which the subject of the reading, the laws of the unconscious, and the historico-cultural determinants are articulated. The importance of this notion of shifter is that it accounts for the process of configuration and for the dynamic aspect of a configuration, rather than for objects and functions. It accounts for the symbolic aspect of exchange. It provides an insight into the problem of the mode of operation of ideology within the built world. It allows us to enter into a mechanism of production of sense that corresponds to an ideology of exchange.

If the system of architecture and of design, even when we play with it, is always closed within a game of commentaries of language—a metalingual game—it is interesting to speculate on the outcome of a similar "game" of *non-design*, a game of the built world. For non-design is a non-language, and by comparison with a language, it is madness since it is outside language, and thus outside society. This non-language, this non-sense constitutes an explosion of the established language in relation to a sense already established (by conventions and repressive rules). It is symbolic of the built world outside the rules of design and their internal "linguistic" games. It permits us finally to understand another logic which informs the significance of building.

The Productive Reading
The outdoor part of the "cafe-terrace" establishes the relationship cafe/street and is organized in terms of the opposition sidewalk as passage or circulation/sidewalk as cafe; another element in the sidewalk-circulation is introduced; people link the first opposition with the second one. Some people walk in the sidewalk/street; some people sit in the sidewalk/cafe. People are distributed in a field of objects that may be distinguished as objects for use and objects for background. Buildings are objects and façades; the background is a continuous façade; the façade of the cafe stands out as a mediating element which because of its transparency creates a relationship between the exterior cafe or cafe/street and the interior cafe. The interior cafe repeats the same oppositions between people/objects and background/mirrors, which themselves now become mediators between exterior and interior in a reflection in which objects, sidewalk, people, street, and interior space are superimposed. . . .

The seats, which are distributed in rows and in which people are clustered, resembles a pit. This substitution produces a point of departure, from cafe/street to cafe/pit.

$$\frac{Cafe\ seats}{Pit\ seats} \times \frac{Pit\ seats}{Theater}$$

$$\frac{Background\ plane\ cafe}{Background\ plane\ scene} \times \frac{Background\ plane\ scene}{Theater}$$

New readings may be produced:

The Gaze:
The gaze from the cafe as pit transforms the street into a scene and sweeps through the codes both of the cafe and the theater. Codes organize the gaze: the people

from whom and to whom they are directed—Observer/Observed; the places from where and to where they are directed—Public/Private; the desire which generates them—Voyeurism/Exhibitionism. In their interrelation, places configurate the gaze: frontal—oblique—sideview. Scene and pit are confused in a general scene where gaze and desire are structured and articulated together. The pleasure in the realization of desire is generated not only at the visual level but also at the level of language in action: that is, discourse.

Discourse within the "theater" is fragmented, dispersed among various actors and spectators, articulating itself without either dominating or subordinating, with the body in action, with the gesture.

Gesture:
Gesticulating bodies form a chain with clothes as a second skin, regulated by the gestures of fashion which play a role in the marking and disguising of sex differences. Cafe, the domain of men, is incorporated in the city as theater, articulated with fashion, the domain of women, as costume. The two together transform the visual codes, which link cafe/masculinity and fashion/femininity, thereby confounding them.

The gesture is not only that of a static pose, but the multiplied gesture of the body in movement, engaged in entries and exits from the scene.

Discourse and gesture configurate the scene; meanwhile, time and volume perforate the plane of decoration and configurate the space.

The scene in the streets:
The scene in the streets is in turn the explosion of the cafe/theater.

The street as a scene of scenes:
The street as a scene of scenes in turn projects into the cafe, opening it up to new paradigms and their codes.

The system of cafes:
Each cafe is not a cafe in itself but is part of a system of cafes, which speaks of its history, of its origins, of its transformations, thus establishing the paradigm of the cafe.

The system of the fragments of public places:
The cafe belongs to the paradigm of streets, plazas, monuments. In turn, each of these is not only physically juxtaposed but also textually juxtaposed. This transforms these places into complex entities: cafe—square, cafe—market, cafe—street. The street is transformed into a new point of departure. We are again in the street, but now the street is a scene.

Street:
A scene in movement. *The street is the scene of struggle, of consumption, the scene of scenes; it is infinitely continuous, unlimited in the motion of objects, of gazes, of gestures.*

It is the scene of history.

It is a scene, but it is also what is behind the scene, *what is not seen, or not allowed to be seen. When what is behind the scene is shown, it produces a demystifying effect, like that of exposing the reasons for the split between individual and social, between private and public.*

The façades *frame the street. They function as scenery or decoration and control the demystifying effect. The decoration may or may not correspond to the content of representation. This accentuates its mask-like character.*

People as decoration:
Fashion transforms people into objects, linking street and theater through one aspect of their common ritual nature.

Rituals:
People meet at corners, people promenade, defining a ritual space, participating in ceremonies, and. . . .

Notes

1. Accordingly, architecture itself must be approached as a particular form of cultural production—as a specific kind of overdetermined practice.

2. Jury Lotman, "Problèmes de la Typologie des Cultures," *Essays in Semiotics*, Kristeva-Reydevobe, ed. (The Hague: Mouton, 1972).

3. See Perouse de Montclos, *Etienne-Louis Boullée* (New York: George Braziller, Inc., 1974); Emil Kaufmann, *Architecture in the Age of Reason* (Cambridge, Mass.: Harvard University Press, 1955).

4. See Christian Metz, *Langage et Cinéma* (Paris: Klincksiek, 1971); Emilio Garroni, *Progetto di Semiotica* (Bari: Laterza, 1973).

5. Ibid.

6. Christian Metz, "Spécificité des Codes et/ou spécificité des langages," *Semiotica*, I, no. 4, 1969.

7. The role of specificity in maintaining the limits of architecture becomes evident, for example, in the development of the steel industry in the nineteenth century, which determined the development of its own independent techniques according to a reason and coherence of its own (exemplified in works of such architects as Eiffel and Paxton), while the world of architectural forces developed according to a logic neatly dissociated from technology. Such technical-formal developments are absorbed through symbolic mechanisms that incorporate the structural system as one of the expressive elements of the architectonic vocabulary. This prevents the fusion of architecture with engineering and its disappearance as an autonomous practice.

8. Heinrich Wölfflin, *Renaissance and Baroque* (Ithaca: Cornell University Press, 1966).

9. René Taylor, "Architecture and Magic: Considerations on the Idea of the Escorial," *Essays in the History of Architecture presented to Rudolf Wittkower*, Douglas Fraser, Howard Hibbard, and Milton J. Lewine, eds. (New York: Phaidon Publishers, Inc., 1967).

10. The notions of closing and opening would allow rethinking of certain aspects of design at the level of meaning in a manner more systematic and specific than the traditional historical analysis that looks for the explanation of the meaning of formal architectural structures in the sociocultural context in general and considers it as a problem of content.

11. Pierre Fontanier, *Les Figures du Discours* (1821) (Paris: Flammarion, 1968).

12. Roman Jakobson, *Studies on Child Language and Aphasia* (The Hague: Mouton, 1971).

13. This is developed by Mario Gandelsonas, "On Reading Architecture," *Progressive Architecture*, May 1972; idem., "Linguistics and Architecture," *Casabella*, 373, Feb. 1973.

14. I refer in this article to the Le Corbusier of *Towards a New Architecture* and *The City of Tomorrow*, although it is possible to say that there are several Le Corbusiers.

15. Le Corbusier, *The City of Tomorrow* (London: John Rodker, 1929).

16. Ibid.

17. Manfredo Tafuri, *Giovan Battista Piranesi; L'Architettura come "Utopia negativa"* (Turin: Accademia delle Scienze, 1972).

18. This articulation has, of course, always been present in architectural treatises from the Renaissance to Le Corbusier. But it is important here, however, to posit it in this functionalist context where the conception of culture is universalist, reductivist, and imperialistic.

19. Alison Smithson, ed., *Team 10 Primer* (Cambridge, Mass.: The MIT Press, 1968).

20. See Diana Agrest and Mario Gandelsonas, "Critical Remarks in Semiotics and Architecture," *Semiotica*, IX, v.3, 1973.

21. Diana Agrest, "Towards a Theory of Production of Sense in the Built Environment," (1968–1973), *On Streets*, Stanford Anderson, ed. (Cambridge, Mass.: The MIT Press, 1972). Here I proposed considering the street as a signifying system.

22. Roland Barthes, *Sade/Fourier/Loyola* (Paris: Editions du Seuil, 1972). See the following works on architectural typology: Garroni, *Progetto di Semiotica*; Giulio Argan, "Sul concetto delle tipologia architettonica," *Progetto e Destino*, Alberto Mondadori, ed. (1965); Aldo Rossi, *L'Architettura della Città* (Padua: Marsilio Editori, 1966); Alan Colquhoun, "Typology and Design Method," *Meaning in Architecture*, Charles Jencks and George Baird, eds. (New York: George Braziller, Inc., 1970), pp. 267–277.

23. See J. J. Goux, *Economie et Symbolique* (Paris: Editions du Seuil, 1973).

24. Roland Barthes, *S/Z* (Paris: Editions du Seuil, 1970).

25. An important difference between the reading of design and non-design is the existence or non-existence of a written text. In the case of design one may reconstruct a discourse in such a way as to illuminate its meaning by a previous reading. When we read Le Corbusier, we reconstruct a reading made by him. In the case of non-design, however, we must put ourselves in the position of direct reading.

26. Tafuri, *Giovan Battista Piranesi.*

27. S. M. Eisenstein, "Piranesi e la fluidità delle forme," *Rassegna Sovietica,* 1–2, 1972.

28. Manfredo Tafuri, "Piranesi, Eisenstein e la dialettica," *Rassegna Sovietica,* 1–2, 1972.

29. Roland Barthes, *The Pleasure of the Text* (New York: Hill and Wang, 1975), p. 49.

30. These nodes, thought of as referents to non-design, permit a more precise formulation of its meaning and distinguish it from the term "place" with which we designate the signifying structure.

31. Roman Jakobson, "Les Catégories verbales et le verbe Russe," *Essais de Linguistique Générale* (Paris: Editions de Minuit); Roland Barthes, *Système de la Mode* (Paris: Editions du Seuil, 1967). The shifter should not be mistaken as being in itself possessed of "double meaning," a notion which has become almost classical in architecture. It does not refer to language. Double meaning, on the contrary, refers to the issue of content, to the problem of ambiguity in relation to language and to metaphor. While the shifter accounts for the chaining of fragments, double meaning refers to a totality with different meanings. There is no chaining and no process involved in this notion.

32. Sigmund Freud, *Interpretation of Dreams* (London: G. Allen & Unwin, Ltd., 1961); idem., *Psychopathology of Everyday Life* (New York: Norton, 1966).

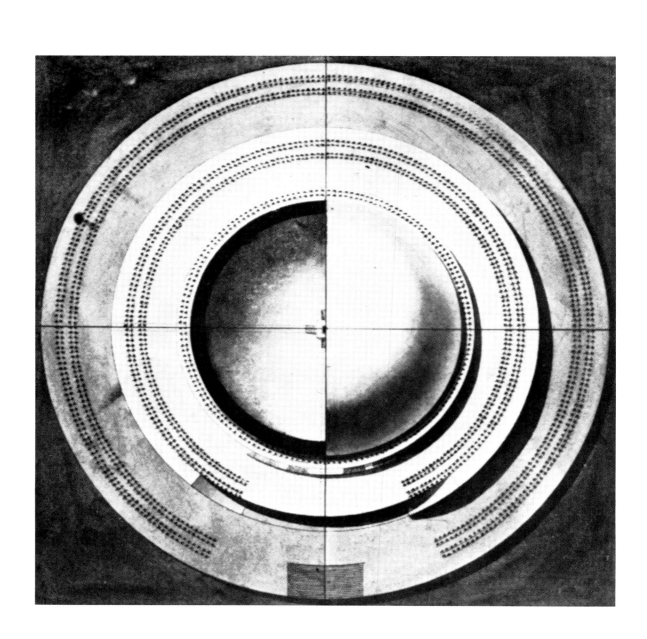

THE MISFORTUNES OF THEORY

The "theory" in this title is a rather ambiguous term encompassing a field formed by diverse texts, some of which can be called theoretical, whereas others fall under the very general category of ideological.

While thinking about the problems that I want to address here, this Sadian title imposed itself with such force that no other could replace it. Virtue can be easily replaced by theory, for what is virtuous in theory, or rather for the virtuosity with which theory would want to be imbued.[1]

Misfortunes refers, in the first part, to a theory marked by a utilitarian conception, determined by the dominant ideology in different periods and that as virtue follows a structure that repeats itself compulsively—a type of functioning of which the form/function relationship provides a good example.

We will see some of the hazards to which this theory will be subjected: abuse, perversion, deceit, etc. For that, the history of the recent past, a moment that in a certain way summarizes the endless chain of misfortunes whose effect is seen/lived as the crisis of architecture, must be studied.

In general, architecture—its history, its theory—is analyzed by considering only its practice, the system on its own, or else by considering it in relation to other fields that determine it (such as economics and politics) or that have been articulated with architecture for centuries (such as the plastic arts).

Translated by Sarah Whiting.

A first hypothesis arising out of this situation is that to understand certain theoretical problems—such as the crisis of architecture—it is necessary today to place architecture in relation to another institutionalized practice that controls and/or regulates the built environment: urban planning.

It is this relating of the two practices that puts into evidence the phenomenon of circulation-migration and the transference of notions and problems from one field to the other. To explore this question, a cut must be made at the moment when urbanism constituted itself as an autonomous practice at the beginning of this century.

Urbanism, in its beginnings, developed as an expansion of architecture in order to resolve the functional problems of the city. Soria y Matta, Ebenezer Howard, and particularly Le Corbusier promoted such an approach.

Urbanism developed as a technique from which a theory will be detached, the "theory" of urbanism. As technique, urbanism is organized around certain problems: social disorder; certain means of solution: form; and a solution: urban plans, urban projects. Also, as with all technical practices, certain norms become necessary for its transmission and will constitute a certain discourse that at a given moment will become autonomous and develop on its own. This discourse will constitute the theories, characterized by instrumentality and empiricism—a type of discourse that crystallizes the ideology of urbanism.[2]

Thanks to this "theoretical" detachment we can notice certain phenomena. The accent that in urbanism was placed on formal propositions, like a response to the serious problems posed by urban development, is going to be shifted in order to be placed on functional aspects: land use, traffic, and transportation. This evolution favors the fusion of urban works with sociological ones, in particular the works on ecology of the Chicago school. The functional sociology of Durkheim and the functional structuralism of Talcott Parsons and his disciples were also included.[3]

Underlying these two discourses—urbanistic and sociological—there is another that structures their "marriage": the general systems theory, which has a double origin: on the one hand, cybernetics, and on the other, biology, represented, respectively, by Norbert Weiner and Ludwig Bertalanffy.[4]

Whereas urbanism, now known as planning, develops more and more, architecture at this point falls into a crisis and struggles to adapt itself to the social demands of the post-World War II era. But let us return to planning.

One of the most relevant aspects of this new planning ideology that begins to crystallize is the replacement of land use in the traditional sense by location theory, incorporating general systems theory. It is mainly location theory that replaces land use in its traditional static approach. A work that is not very well known but that was very influential is "The Core of the City," by Walter Isard and John Rannells, which exemplified this change.

In this line one should mention the classic work of Stuart Chapin, *Land Use Planning*, and that of Donald Foley, which in a more conventional way develops a descriptive model of relationships between value systems, activity systems, and physical characteristics in an urban context in space and in a temporal process.[5]

Another related approach is that of applying the theory of communications in planning. Works such as *Communications Theory of Urban Growth* by Richard Meier and *Community Without Propinquity* and *Urban Place and the Non-Place Urban Realm* by Melvin Webber, among others, are representative of this approach.

These new approaches that develop in planning will in turn influence architecture, which will place the accent on the functional aspects, now called "activity systems." A new series of notions such as communications, mobility, and flexibility and a series of other notions associated with the idea of progress enter the architectural discourse. The works of Cedric Price, Archigram, etc., are illustrative of this.

The planning theory that has an instrumental origin thus has as a final goal its application, that is, a technique.[6] If previously it was theory that did not conform to urban problems—and therefore one needed a theory, a carefully constructed ideology—now it is technique that no longer conforms to the needs of a society that becomes harder and harder to keep in "equilibrium." A society, an urban milieu, that manifests more and more the contradictions of planning in the capitalist system in its monopolist stage. It is the period of models. Planning models already existed, but they did not have a central role. Now it is the models that are going to impose themselves, not only as technique, but as theory itself.

There are many examples of developments in this domain: the work of Ira Lowry, a model of models; Britton Harris, who presents the models in an already famous issue of the journal of American Institute of Planners, Jay Forrester, etc. The writings of this last author are exemplary. His *Urban Dynamics* is one of the most sophisticated works to appear in recent years from the point of view of the application of systems theory. The goal of the study is to prevent urban deterioration and to project the renewal of already deteriorated zones. It is what one could call a predictive, projective model that presents itself nonetheless as an urban theory. To quote: "This model *is* a theory." (italics mine). It is interesting to note that Forrester worked in industry and that his earlier book, *Industrial Dynamics*, served as a model for *Urban Dynamics*.[7]

Technical as they are, these models also have a teleological structure, but they present themselves nonetheless as theories. That, precisely, is their ideological effect, which covers its true political role with the apparent neutrality of theory.

Once again architecture, in search of its lost object, is contaminated by this model fever. Christopher Alexander is already a precursor, and models now can be seen everywhere. They become the architectural avant-garde, bringing a kind of scientific guarantee given the tool of mathematics (which though science in its own domain become techniques when applied elsewhere—a phenomenon little understood by those who believe in a sort of osmosis whereby architecture, through the application of mathematical models, can itself become a science).[8]

These travels, these comings and goings from architecture to urbanism and from urbanism to architecture, can be understood from the point of view of architecture itself—that is, its ideology, beyond direct economic explanations (which certainly exist)—as another version of the oscillation between the two poles: that of form and that of function, an oscillation that now, instead of taking place within the field of architecture, passes to an amplified field of intervention in the environment, the urban realm.

The loss of the architectural object is one of the effects of these comings and goings. Architecture becomes a pure program in a situation that can be characterized as a fiction, an illusion. An example of this is found in the work of Cedric Price, who, influenced by the theories of planning, is interested fundamentally in activity systems, form no longer being a pertinent problem. Hence in a university project it is his contention that what is needed is not an "architectural" design but rather the design of the activity system itself. This does not seem like a bad idea, but in fact the architect as such has no power of intervention in this domain. Because form no longer interests the architect, and his intervention in activity systems is but an illusion, the architect, caught in the form/function dichotomy, loses his object.

And as in the misfortunes, when architecture finally finds theory within the domain of planning, she will die like Justine, killed by a lightning bolt when she regains virtue (at the house of her sister, who represents perversion and thus the death of virtue).

The unfortunate transfers of notions from one field to another can also be understood in light of the displacement between the dominant ideology (economic, in the form of technocracy) and this subregion of ideology (architecture).[9]

Le Corbusier represents the moment at which the ideological dominance corresponds to the juro-political region. His plans, his propositions, his projects adapt themselves very well to the needs of the established system from the political and ideological points of view. It is the ideology that he, better than any other architect, develops; his *plan regulateur, plan directeur,* his visionary projects—in brief, the form of the systemization of this ideology—corresponds to this period.

If this is the form that corresponds to this dominant juro-political ideology in its architectural subregion at the moment of capitalist monopolism whose dominant ideology is that of economy in the form of technocracy, then the architectural ideology influenced by technocracy through planning is that of communication, of interaction.[10] Immateriality becomes a preeminent notion—systems over form, over physical configurations, over architectural space. The form that corresponds to this ideology is that of models, of programs elaborated with very sophisticated techniques; thus the form that corresponds to the preceding period no longer functions, and when attempts are made to keep this form, they are short lived, as in the case of Archigram where the mode of systematizing ideology can be seen as similar to that of Le Corbusier, whereas the ideology it represents is that of a later period.

Le Corbusier represents a moment of conflict within the social structure at the moment of its passage from one stage to another, a conflict that is produced within, at the moment of change, and is manifested in architecture in the oscillation between form and function—a causalist circle where formalism or economicism (functionalism) are some of the results—which does not allow one to see the real contradictions that exist not between those two levels but within each of them.

In this sense, a virtue of the development of the models is its extreme character, by which its economic and political role—in relation to the architect—becomes explicit.

From this situation, it seems clear enough that there are basically two fields for theoretical work (which dominate all others): the economic and the symbolic (semiotic), the latter the domain of production and transformation of sense, the domain of the ideological. Both situate themselves in relation to politics, to the condition of its production.

The goal of this separation into semiotic and economic is to respect the pertinent levels of theoretical intervention. This separation makes possible a theoretical work in a domain (the semiotic) that has its own specific logic and that cannot be explained in a direct and general form by another—by the economic domain. By semiotics, we mean ideology as the production of sense, and architecture (as ideology from this point of view) as a specific production of sense.[11]

In this light a change of the level of the architectural problematic is insinuated, on one hand because we have an object defined as the theoretical object, on the other hand because this same object is situated outside of or beyond the theoretical trap that the form/function relationship represents.

Even though it seems that the misfortunes end here, this end is only the beginning of another series and the beginning of a new chapter.

To think of architecture (and by this I mean the practice of building) as symbolic, or to think of the built as symbolic, necessitates some clarification in relation to an alternative with which we are confronted, that of developing an architectural semiotics from the point of view of communication—or else, of "opening within the interior of the communication perspective another question, that of the production of sense," which is "not equivalent to communication, even though it is produced by it."[12] This should be understood in relation to the difference between the problematic of exchange and that of (productive) work.

This question of the relationship between communication and production will define the new misfortunes. Once again, we will refer to the communication approach to planning, an important reference, for it has influence on architecture. These works are very close to the problem of signification, but do not get to touch upon it.[13]

Even if the domains of communication and signification are tightly linked, there is a radical difference between these two terms. Of the elements of the communication model used by Meier and Webber—sender, receiver, channel, and information—two are emphasized or, rather, considered: the channel and the quantity of information. Sender and receiver are considered only in terms of origin and goal. The channel becomes the fundamental element in terms of transporting information. It is thus that they avoid entering into the nature of the information communicated, that is, the message, the language of which these messages are part; above all, they do not enter into the problem of the structure of codes that makes this communication possible. The theoretical implications of the notions of code and of message do not seem to be understood; the potential of a complete model and, in particular, of elements such as message and code, are ignored.

The analysis of the *nature* of the system of signs (signification) should be different from its *use* in communication, which is the only aspect to be considered by the cited planning theories (in relation to channel and information). It is from the notion of the code, the most important element in the communication model, that the study of the nature of a signifying system may be approached. An element that is excluded from those communication theories due to certain ideological obstacles is to be found in the double origin of these theories.

On one hand, concerning urbanism and urban design, these theories continue the tradition—with transformations, of course—based on the functionalist approach of urban architectural models. On the other hand, they introduce notions of social science, of sociology and social psychology, to solve the "nonphysical" problems of the environment. Here too, the tradition is that of functionalism in the social sciences,[14] a functionalism that implies in architecture a causalistic relationship between the poles of form and function, a universal conception for which any form is the result of function and a naturalist conception in the search for the form that will "ideally" adapt to function.

These same conditions—causalism, universalism, utilitarianism, among others—are also characteristic of the functionalism in the social sciences.[15] This functionalism becomes the obstacle preventing the development of the notion of code that allows the understanding, for example, of the form/function relationship as only one of the structural links that determine the signifying nature of the environment.

The use of an incomplete model of communication is the result of an operation by which the elements of the model that would conflict with a functional utilitarianist approach such as message and code are eliminated.

Similarly, when entering the semiotic domain, the phantom of functionalism reappears as a residue of the functionalism that produced the situation we described in the first series of misfortunes. Once again, the subversion of the notion of function seems necessary. As for the misfortunes, if we think that in shifting from communication to signification we are relieved from all misfortunes, we will see that this is not always the case.

A first step in opposition to the work already cited is to consider the urban environment as signification in terms of a culture that produces objects. The project of considering the environment as signification is confronted with at least two different options. One is "to approach the systems of signification, as structured by communication, that is, by the transmission and exchange of messages that take place by the exchange of signs in a play within the interior of the sign"—signifier/signified—and fundamentally between signs.[16]

The economic metaphor de Saussure uses to describe the linguistic value as an exchange between things (work and salary), or as a comparison of similar things (five dollars with ten dollars, or five dollars with twenty-five francs), allows for the understanding of this operation.[17]

A series of works begins to develop thus within this line but in general reproduces the established architectural categories in semiotic terms (without entering in the problem of the production of sense: a second option).

In the past few years of the analysis of sense, the ideological limitations of such an approach to signification have become clear.[18]

Another option is that of envisaging the signification in relation to the possibilities initiated by the critique of economics and by the accent that such a critique has put on the notion of productive work or production.

The analysis of production allows the development of the critique of a system based on the exchange and circulation of a product. A critique, in the same direction, was developed in semiotics, analyzing the circulation of signs in a similar manner.[19] It has been said that at the level of society, language functions like money in that it permits the exchange of information but hides the production of meaning (sense). It is thus that we see the two options mentioned above: either to formalize semiotic systems within the perspective of the exchange and circulation of signs (semiology from the point of view of communication), or to enter in the problematics of the production of sense preceding sense.[20] Even if we can already see the difficulties inherent to such an enterprise, the risk seems worth taking. It is within this option that I place myself.

Signification, therefore, is not seen as that which the "thing"—architecture, the urban environment—communicates (as a problem of context), but as the operations of production of sense within determined social and historic conditions.

From this perspective, one must consider not only the historic conditions of the production of sense but also a productive subject. It is not the case of a psychological subject who situates himself as an individual facing the world; it is the subject of the unconscious, which in following its own laws, its own logic, will leave its marks in the production.

The urban environment is thus considered an articulation of different codes and matters. The analysis of these codes from this perspective is not a classification of an inventory that finds a series of rules and regularities. The codes are like forces within a dynamic process that produce and transform the sense in relation to determined conditions of production. How can these forces be studied without reducing them to a system, to a closed construction? It is the articulation of codes, more than the codes themselves, that interests us.

If the analysis, from the point of view of the communication of sense (traditional semiotics) is based on the principle of unity that permits the recognition of similarities and differences (value), which in turn reinforces the functionalist ideology in architecture, then what guides the work I now propose, which begins by a work of reading, is the principle of dispersion.[21] The complexity, the heterogeneity that accepts contradiction as a constitutive part, must be retained in opposition to the unifying reductionism that eliminates them. Rather than closing the system— characteristic of architecture—this principle opens it, permitting thus the articulation of many readings, signifying chains.

The reading is conceived as a process of chaining, which constitutes a structuring force. The multiplication of sense produced by the readings, by the infinite chains of signifiers, by this explosion of sense, makes us enter a new dynamic space similar to the work of the dream, that of the production of sense.[22]

We could think of this articulation of readings as that which is the movement of sense, as that which permits us to enter into the exchange of the system and allows us to think of a practice based on a work on such mechanisms. It would be the reading as "redesign," which can blur the boundaries between theory, critique, and practice.

Notes

1. I refer here to *Les Infortunes de la Vertu* by Marquis de Sade.

2. Louis Althusser, Etienne Balibar, *Lire le Capital* (Paris: François Maspero, 1967); Michel Pecheux, "Ideologie et Histoire des Sciences," in Fichaut Pecheux, *Sur L'Histoire des Sciences* (Paris: François Maspero, 1969).

3. Talcott Parsons, *Essays in Sociological Theory. The Structure of Social Action* (New York: McGraw-Hill, 1937); Louis Wirth, *On Cities and Social Life* (Chicago: University of Chicago Press, 1964).

4. Norbert Wiener, *Cybernetics* (New York: John Wiley & Sons, 1948); W. Ross Ashby, *An Introduction to Cybernetics* (London: Chapman & Hall, 1956); Ludwig von Bertalanffy, *General Systems Theory* (New York: George Braziller, 1969).

5. Melvin M. Webber, *Order in Diversity, Community without Propinquity in Cities and Space* (Baltimore: Johns Hopkins University Press, 1963); idem., "The Urban Place and the Non-Place Urban Realm," in *Explorations into Urban Structure* (Philadelphia: University of Pennsylvania Press, 1964); Richard Meier, *A Communication Theory of Urban Growth* (Cambridge, Mass.: MIT Press, 1962); F. Stuart Chapin, *Urban Land Use Planning* (Urbana: University of Illinois Press, 1965); J. Brian McLoughlin, *Urban and Regional Planning. A Systems Approach* (London: Faber and Faber, 1969); Donald Foley, "An Approach to Metropolitan Spatial Structure," in *Explorations into Urban Structure.*

6. Althusser, *Lire le Capital.*

7. F. Stuart Chapin, "A Model for Simulating Residential Development," in *Journal of the American Institute of Planners*, special issue, *Urban Development Models: New Tools for Planning*, Britton Harris, guest ed., vol. 31, no. 2 (May 1965); Jay Forrester, *Urban Dynamics* (Cambridge, Mass.: MIT Press, 1969); Alain Badiou, *Le Concept de Modèle* (Paris: François Maspero, 1969).

8. Christopher Alexander, *Notes on the Synthesis of Form* (Cambridge, Mass.: Harvard University Press, 1964).

9. Nicos Poulantzas, *Pouvoir Politique et Classes Sociales de l'Etat Capitaliste* (Paris: François Maspero, 1968); Manuel Castells, *La Question Urbaine* (Paris: François Maspero, 1968).

10. Poulanzas, *Pouvoir Politique*; Louis Althusser, "Sur le Travail Théorique, Difficultés et Ressources," *La Pensée* 132 (April 1967).

11. Julia Kristeva, "La Semiologie Comme Science Sociale et/ou Critique de la Science," in *Théorie d'Ensemble* (Paris: Editions du Seuil, 1968).

12. Ibid.

13. Meier, *A Communication Theory*; Webber, *Order in Diversity*, "The Urban Place."

14. Parsons, *Essays in Sociological Theory*; Wirth, *On Cities and Social Life.*

15. Ibid.; Thomas Herbert, "Theoretical Practice and Social Sciences," and "Notes for a General Theory of Ideology," in *Proceso Ideologico*, ed. Eliseo Yenon (Buenos Aires: Editions Tiempo Contemporaneo, 1971).

16. Kristeva, "La Semiologie."

17. Ferdinand de Saussure, *Course in General Linguistics* (New York: McGraw-Hill, 1966).

18. Kristeva, "La Semiologie"; Jacques Derrida, *De la Grammatologie* (Paris: Editions de Minuit, 1967).

19. Ibid.

20. Kristeva, "La Semiologie."

21. Roland Barthes, *S/Z* (Paris: Editions du Seuil, 1970).

22. Ibid.

ARCHITECTURAL ANAGRAMS:
THE SYMBOLIC PERFORMANCE OF SKYSCRAPERS

This text focuses on the skyscraper in relation to the logic of its signifying functioning, an analysis which allows us not only to discuss issues that touch on the crisis of meaning in architecture but also to identify certain mechanisms of the production of meaning hitherto ignored by architectural criticism.

An adequate definition of the skyscraper—both as a type and as an object of study—is well established among historians and critics of architecture. Numerous histories and critical appraisals have focused on the problem of determining those characteristics of the skyscraper which would enable the first building of that type to be identified.[1] While structural technique and the elevator were initially decisive in determining the original appearance of the type, these were soon overwhelmed by the factor of height. These attributes of technique, elevator, and scale do not, however, account for an equally critical aspect of the skyscraper's development, namely the problem of meaning.

In his book *The History of Skyscrapers*, Francisco Mujica coined the term "Neo-American" architecture and argued that the Mayan pyramid, whose form was echoed in the setback building profile of the 1920s, could be seen as the first skyscraper. While Herbert Croly wrote about the scenographic nature of the skyscraper, Montgomery Schuyler proposed that the determining criteria for a new history of the skyscraper should be formal or typological rather than technical, functional, or economic in nature. Schuyler's proposition was followed by that of W. Weisman, whose typological study of the history of the skyscraper recognized

The City of the Future: Hundred-Story City in Neo-American Style. Francisco Mujica, architect, 1930.

seven phases, from the first or pre-skyscraper to the most recent architectural expression. Broadly speaking, Weisman's phases were established as follows: phase 1. pre-skyscraper (1849–1870); phase 2. initial evolution (1858–1870); phase 3. transition from mansard to flat roof (after 1878); phase 4. evolution of the tripartite composition (after 1880); phase 5. evolution of the tower (1888–1895); phase 6. the setback block (after 1916); and phase 7. evolution of the superblock (after 1930).[2]

Starting with the tripartite form posited by Weisman as being characteristic of phase 4, we will examine the transposition of meaning that occurs as the type evolves from phase 5 to phase 7. In the following analysis of the structure of meaning in skyscraper form, we shall restrict ourselves solely to the following three aspects: 1) the problem of eclecticism, that is, the recourse to diverse styles or modes such as the Gothic, Beaux-Arts, etc.; 2) the skyscraper's characteristic tripartite structure: base, shaft, and capital or crest; and 3) the relationship between the various parts of this "column."

The problem of eclecticism takes us back to a dominant feature of the skyscraper's origin: that is, its double signifying aspect, which manifests itself first as being relative to architecture and to architectural codes, and second as being related to other elements in the city. Both of these relationships, participating in a different kind of signifying functioning, are condensed and unified in the single architectonic object. This phenomenon allows one to think about the function of meaning in architecture as a signifying super-position rather than a simple, singular meaning.

Although the tripartite-columnar character of the skyscraper was characterized as only an intermediate stage in the history of its evolution, it is a type of configuration that still prevails either in a latent or manifest form in high-rise building types of a later date. The tripartite analogy to the column, the architectural signifier par excellence,[3] appears in different forms in every architectural period. Buildings as columns were already being projected in the Enlightenment in, for example, the column house of the Desert de Retz near Marly by de Monville, where the building, a column in ruins, is both column and ruin. In the case of the skyscraper, its columnar form evokes a nonexistent historical past and prefigures a city in ruins,

Havermeyer Building, New York City.
George P. Post, architect, 1891–1892.
Tripartite type.

which, like the ruins of the Roman Forum, is to be transformed into a city of columns, or rather megacolumns in this particular case.

The Chicago Tribune competition[4] demonstrates this kind of primary myth in the various "column" entries (the most well-known being that of Adolf Loos, which posits itself as a direct and ironic symbolization of the building as column). The functional structural element raised in this way to a symbolic position indicates the inevitable signifying existence of the element "column" itself, as well as the apparent contradiction between the symbolism and the technique. But what is it that the skyscraper as column supports? In Egyptian temples, the columns held up a painted sky ceiling.[5] This precise metaphor is repeated in one of the projects for the Chicago Tribune: P. Gerhard's building in the form of an Egyptian column reminds us that skyscrapers are in effect columns supporting the sky.

The development of each part of the column—base, shaft, and capital—accounts for this signifying transformation in the skyscraper, the base/capital-crest relation-

Project by Paul Gerhard.

Project by Matthew Freeman.

ship returning us to the problem of architecture as a metalanguage. The upper terminal of the skyscraper, often designed as an exemplar of an individual building in itself, makes a commentary on the architecture absent in the base, thereby developing a parallel discourse which speaks about the fundamental contradiction of all architecture, namely, form versus function or art versus technique.

Eclecticism

Gothic, Roman, and Beaux-Arts styles serve as metaphors linking the new to the old and imposing something new by means of the familiar. These institutionalized forms make a certain acceptance possible, just as the trips to the moon in early science fiction films were filtered through the ideology of the period in order to transform fiction into verisimilitude. Even though the skyscraper is an achievable reality in technological terms, it is only acceptable if as a metaphor it has the capacity to represent at one and the same time past values (through the architectural styles) and the prevailing values of the time (progress). This displacement between technical development and the formal typology adopted, or the different architec-

Project by I. N. Phelps Stokes.

Project by Lossow and Kühne.

Winning project by Raymond Hood.

tural modes or styles, arises out of a more fundamental displacement between the economic and ideological levels which develop in different times and thus have no simple one-to-one correspondence. The inertia of formal ideology relative to the other levels is made manifest by the fact that while structural technique keeps pace with "technological utopia," stylistic ideology remains rooted in some earlier period. This implies that economic considerations are incapable of directly determining the formal aspect.

The consequent separation of the skyscraper into two aspects—the structural and the symbolic—as represented by the façade treatment implies not only a certain reduction in formal emphasis to allow for the development of technique,[6] but furthermore stresses the signifying independence, the mask-like character, inherent in all façades and the scenographic nature of the architectural object.

From the outset, the skyscraper was conceived as a symbolic object in its totality—irrespective of the particular symbolism associated with its stylistic characteristics.

Project by Eliel Saarinen, second prize.

Late submission by Claes Oldenburg, 1965.

The conventionality of the styles, which became manifest with eclecticism, was symptomatic not so much of a de-ideologization of architecture but rather of its re-ideologization.

Within the entire group of entries for the Chicago Tribune competition we can identify two fundamental operations that demonstrate this process, operations that relate to style and established codes. On the one hand, a metalinguistic operation appears in a number of the competition entries as a critical device, which undermines the received tradition of architecture. On the other hand, a connotative operation is present in other projects as a mechanism for absorption and assimilation, which reinforces the established principles or codes of architecture. Thus, while some of the entries in the contest are metalinguistically ironic and sometimes cynical in attitude or effect, the winning entry by Howells and Hood, like its predecessor, the Woolworth Building by Cass Gilbert, is typically connotative of the Gothic now endowed with associations of splendor and wealth. This "Neo-Gothic" style is a manner which allowed for the evolutionary development of the present-day skyscraper, and indicates the struggle of language with its connotative possibilities against the explosive metalinguistic potential of eclecticism. Eclecticism thus provides the means for an ideological transformation of architecture in order to create a new vocabulary, a new language necessary for the consolidation of a new ideology.

The program for the Chicago Tribune competition emphasized the formal and visual over the technological aspect, in this way evidently searching to formulate a new typology, a quest which was to a certain extent successful.

The skyscraper plays an important role not only in terms of technological development and as a new manifestation of the ideology of free enterprise, competition, and consumption (that is, as a typology which is pertinent to that global ideology) but also in relation to architectural ideology itself, that is, in relation to the *production* of meaning in architecture.

Critics[7] have emphasized the pragmatic nature of eclecticism in American architecture, that is, the application of styles independent of their intrinsic meaning (if such existed) or of the function of the building as a product of individual initiative in the capitalist city. Such an application of styles may also represent a consciousness that the apparent isolation in which each building is conceived is in reality fictitious. If eclecticism, developed as a more or less coherent style in the nineteenth century, originally had the critical role of demonstrating the arbitrariness of the relation between form and meaning, then the pragmatic eclecticism of the twentieth-century skyscraper fulfills a dual role. On the one hand, in relation to the building itself, it shows the nonintrinsic or arbitrary character of meaning; on the other hand, in relation to the building in the city, it demonstrates that meaning is a relation of value—as physical and conceptual contiguity—which arises when architecture is considered as an urban element and not as a single monument. This double role might seem paradoxical insofar as each skyscraper *is* treated by itself as a monument. The monumentality of the skyscraper, however, does not reside in the building itself, but rather in the process by which symbolic interrelationships are established between buildings and between these buildings and urban places. This totality, which is eclectic, does no more than reflect what architecture, with its emphasis on unity and its denial of context, tends to repress. The skyscraper reveals the necessarily eclectic nature of semiplanned urban growth and provides an explicit typology which by its nature allows for a complex combinatory and transformational game. The Chicago Tribune competition, at the same time as it manifests this double effect of meaning in relation to the building and to the urban totality, reveals the symbolic aspect to be different from the stylistic one.

Manhattan itself may be seen as the combination of several typologies that intersect with each other in their original development and in their later evolution as fragments of a nonexistent language. Manhattan functions as an explosion of meaning and design which puts architecture into crisis. Skyscrapers are scattered fragments of that explosion, their diffusion and their differing trajectories departing from a common origin. Explosion, puzzle, anagram—each of these metaphors makes us think of both fragmentation and unity since any recomposition implies a high degree of randomness. Each stage in the typological development of the skyscraper reverberates spatially in the urban whole. The crests as signifying elements—the small buildings, the setback, and the telescopic pinnacle—appear with variations in scale and proportion in nearly all buildings, not only in skyscrapers. The traditional styles persist even when new ones appear. The inertia of eclecticism has thus allowed Manhattan to become at record pace a city with a much longer history than that which it truly possesses—a miracle of instant history! But of course such instant history cannot be thought of in the same manner as the history of architecture has traditionally been understood, insofar as the superimposition of the diachronic (or temporal) and the synchronic (or instant) axes create a specific kind of signifying functioning. This juxtaposition of different meanings, operating simultaneously in a nonlinear fashion, makes the skyscraper a signifier within a discourse which is anagrammatic in both the literal and poetic sense.[8]

Skyscrapers manifest a process of symbolization that is almost independent of the architect himself: this process extends beyond the analysis of the building as a sign, beyond what is communicated by the depth of its meaning or content, and makes accessible the structures that account for the possible conditions of its symbolic functioning. The skyscraper is an empty signifier that can assume and attract different meanings.

The Tripartite Structure

The analysis of the skyscraper as a tripartite structure informs its syntactic and semantic transformation in relation to the signifying functioning described above. The three elements of the column—the analogical origin of the skyscraper's form—are always present and undergo successive modification as a consequence of their interrelationship. The three phases of the skyscraper's evolution, which according to Weisman follow the tripartite phase, are marked by the development of specific relations existing between base and capital or between base and shaft—and the later evolution of both "base" and "capital" into buildings in their own right.[9]

Crests

Alfred Bossom choosing a crest for the top of a skyscraper that has already been designed, 1934.

In the first decade of this century, the body of the skyscraper became transformed into a base for the crest. The body was increasingly regularized or simplified while the crest was increasingly articulated and assumed a symbolic dimension denoting the exchange value of the building. These crests with their scenic and panoramic nature were both a public and publicity element operating at the scale of the whole city. There was no limit set for the height of the skyscraper according to the zoning regulations: yet this question of height was to be a concern of architects for a long time. How should one mark such a limit symbolically? Was the upper transition equal to a completion or something entirely different? This relationship was expressed by Montgomery Schuyler in "The Towers of Manhattan": "the practical requirements in every case issue, as to the body of the building, in an almost identical result, that is to say, a parallelopiped with the minimum of supports or 'solids' and the maximum of 'voids' or windows. It is only in the skyline, in the upper termination that he [the architect] has as an artist a real chance." This is exemplified in a photograph in which architect and critic Alfred Bossom appears to be trying out alternative crests for the body of a skyscraper which he has already designed.[10]

In this type of selection, a play of architectonic codes can be seen to occur independently from the rest of the building, producing a parallel architecture in which each termination is a building in itself executed in a self-contained style. These parallel architectures set up a game in which the signifiers are liberated, united, opposed, repeated, and quoted, generating a metalinguistic discourse, which su-

The Chicago Tribune Competition, 1924.
Project by Franklin James Hunt.

Project by Huestis and Huestis.

Project by Milnar Chapman Markes.

Project by J. D. Leland and Company.

Project by Frank Fort.

perimposes an invisible net on the city—marked by the grid of the streets to which the base relates. On first examination this relationship between the shaft or body and the crest or capital might be interpreted simplistically as a manifestation of a contradiction in which the *technical* aspect of the body may be regarded as being opposed to the *symbolic* aspect of the crest, the two apparently irreconcilable aspects tending, according to a functional hypothesis, to negate each other to such degree as to make the symbolic disappear. If the skyscraper is analyzed in its urban context, however, such a direct opposition dissolves.

The relationships between buildings are complex insofar as they are established not only in terms of entire buildings or of the building's body to its crest, but also in terms of relations between crest and crest, and between the body of one building and the crest of another, etc. The Chicago Tribune competition demonstrates clearly the importance of the crest in the imagery of the skyscraper, to such an extent that in many cases the crest becomes the building itself. The transformations by which the crest cedes its symbolic role first to the entire building and then to the base can be exemplified by three instances: the "spires" of the St. Mark's and Price towers by Frank Lloyd Wright; Hugh Ferriss's setback skyscraper where the whole building becomes a crest; and finally the case where the body or shaft be-

Chrysler Building under construction. Drawing by Hugh Ferriss, 1929.

Chrysler Building as built. William Van Alen, architect, 1929.

comes the whole building, thereby eliminating the symbolic crest entirely. The last case is really a mutation of the first, in which the building as crest is transformed into a base thereby foreclosing one transformation and opening the next.

The law that established the need for the setback—a requirement which Le Corbusier rightly regarded as romantic—unconsciously paid homage to one of the most characteristic aspects of the skyscraper, namely its upward transition toward a point of culmination. This characteristic can be observed beginning with the tripartite phase and continuing through all its successive manifestations. The Chrys-

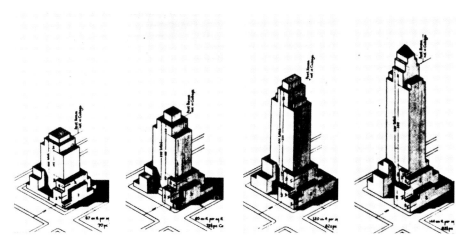

Building "setback" envelopes, 1916.

Chrysler Building as built. William Van Alen, architect, 1929.

Empire State Building. Drawing by Hugh Ferriss, 1929.

ler Building, unequaled in its elaboration and fantasy, touching the sky through its scintillating reflection, seems to be the apotheosis of this transition in which the whole building has become the symbol of the skyscraper itself. By contrast, its complement, the Empire State Building, is an empty signifier remaining always in transition, never completely coming to a point of culmination. The Empire State Building, like the Eiffel Tower, is looked at only in terms of its own gaze, as the prime vantage point from which, as its name would indicate, New York reveals itself.

Zoning envelopes, 1929. Evolution of the   *Second stage.*
setback building. Drawings by Hugh
Ferriss. First stage.

Third stage.

Fourth stage.

Under the setback law, then, the building replicates the crest at another scale (a characteristic operation in designing crests). Hugh Ferriss's drawings of the "code envelopes"—just like the buildings on Park Avenue between Fifty-third and Forty-fifth streets—are revealing in this sense.

The relationships in this circulation of meanings can be considered as in the manner of the following diagram: By means of the circulation of meanings, the shaft of the building emerges as the one element that engenders another form of symbolic functioning in the skyscraper. The meaningful relationship now becomes the space between the buildings, and their repetition now becomes the essential aspect of meaning. This is clear in the World Trade Center, where the "tallest building" is actually two buildings, and the crest as a symbol has been metonymically replaced by a double aspect: repetition and the space between considered as form in itself.[11] The relation of value is here manifested as basic in the determination of meaning in architecture.

Buildings in the Modeling. *Drawing by*
Hugh Ferriss, 1929.

Diagrams showing formal transformations
and circulation of meanings in the evolution
of the type. Original drawings by Diana
Agrest, © *1974.*

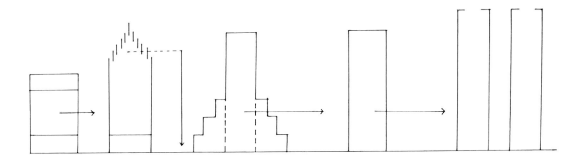

*Bricken Building, New York City. Ely
Jacques Kahn, architect, c. 1930.*

*500 Fifth Avenue, New York City. Shreve,
Lamb & Harmon, architects, 1930.*

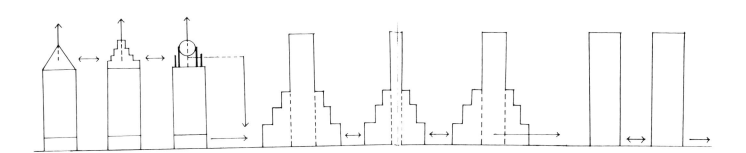

The Base

We have already noted how the signifying functioning of the skyscraper may be understood in terms of its underlying tripartite structure considered as the equivalent of the classical column. In the transformation of the relationships among the elements of the column, a stage is reached in which the base takes on the symbolic role, thus marking a point in the evolution of a new typology of the skyscraper.

The base as a "door" establishes the relationship of the building to the street, thereby assuming the role of the public realm of the skyscraper. Thus in the Chrysler Building the ground floor is treated in a monumental way both in scale and in detail. The door, that major signifier throughout the history of architecture, marks the entry as the mediator between public and private, but also between the architectonic public realm and that realm which is nonarchitectonic, between architecture and nonarchitecture. The base as a door in relation to the street activates a series of signifiers of public space. In this process, two tendencies have developed, one which displaces the public aspect of the building to its exterior by the use of plazas, which also amplify the perspective space, and a second which develops the base as an enlarged entrance where the building instead of expanding outward is perforated and opened up.

The Displaced Base

The development of the first tendency, the displacement of the public realm to the exterior, is pioneered by the Rockefeller Center and culminates in the Seagram Building by Mies van der Rohe and Philip Johnson. The latter is the precedent for the relationships between building and plaza recently perpetuated in the new series of skyscrapers on Sixth Avenue.[12] In these, the plazas have the function of providing a transition between the designed, public outside realm and the nondesigned, public outside realm, thus preserving the hermetic character of the building. This space acts as a reference to the traditional space around monumental public buildings: a space provided for the public to meditate upon the power enclosed in the building. In Rockefeller Center this plaza-promenade acts as a doorway for the entire complex. The use of the giant door or gate as a fundamental signifying element reaches its extreme in the World Trade Center where the two towers themselves take the form of a "door," thus transforming themselves into a gateway to the city which is clearly visible from both Staten Island and New

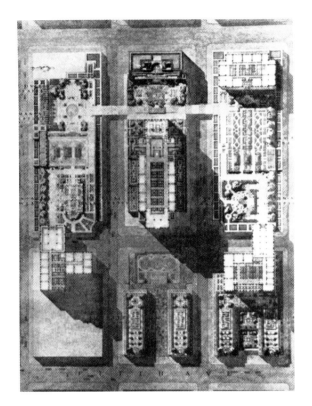

Rockefeller Center, New York City.
Reinhard and Hofmeister; Corbett,
Harrison, and MacMurray; and Hood,
Godley, and Fouilhoux, architects, 1932.
Plan.

General view. Drawing by Martin Wenrich,
1923.

*I. D. S. Building, Minneapolis. Philip
Johnson and John Burgee, architects, 1972.*

*World Trade Center, New York City.
K. Yamasaki, architect, 1976. The towers
take the form of a door to the city.*

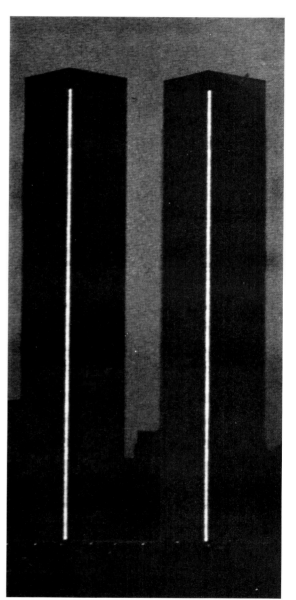

Jersey; that is to say, from the principal access points to the great metropolis. A "doorway" as high as infinity, the point where the parallels intersect . . . it is hardly an accident that this metaphor should be developed in a time of invisible communication.

Rockefeller Center was not only a pioneer in the treatment of the exterior space, but also initiated the change in emphasis in the functioning of the base, from the primacy of exterior public space to the volume of public space interpenetrating the building itself. This last is the megastructural character toward which today's skyscrapers increasingly tend.

The Building as Base—A Mutant Species

In this second kind of transformation, the base, formerly a secondary signifier, undergoes an unusual transformation in which the entrance hall gradually emerges as a principal element. This transformation marks the latest stage of the skyscraper's development, in which the skyscraper mutates toward a new typology of which partial examples already exist: the I. D. S. Center at Minneapolis by Philip Johnson, John Burgee, and Edward Baker, a "fifty-seven-story tower higher and larger than seven tennis courts";[13] the Pennzoil Place in Houston by the same architects; a series of Hyatt Hotels by John Portman and Associates; and the Ford Foundation Building in New York by Kevin Roche and John Dinkeloo.

In these examples one can see the way in which the entry hall becomes a fundamental element. Its size is physically increased so that in the most extreme case of Portman's buildings, it becomes the medula of the building, producing a fundamental inversion by which the public aspect is incorporated into the private area. The base thus becomes the building itself from within. In Johnson's work the public space is closed off and incorporated into the building as a continuation of the street, but the base is still differentiated from the body of the building. In the Ford Foundation, the entire building becomes a door, but the urban imagery evident in the work of Johnson and Portman is absent. This building seems to be transitional between the work of Portman and the plazas on Sixth Avenue. These examples contain the germs of a current problematic which is about to produce change in architecture at the typological and conceptual levels and anticipate the emergence of a totally new type of which utopistic versions have already appeared—the mega-

Ford Foundation Building, New York City. Kevin Roche and John Dinkeloo, architects, 1976. The entry takes the full height of the building.

Overhead Traffic Ways. *Drawing by Hugh Ferriss, 1929.*

structure, a form that will resolve in itself as a type the contradiction between city and architecture, design and nondesign.[14] In this type, the building is infiltrated by the irresistible forces of the city and by signifiers that have hitherto only surrounded it.

This city-skyscraper relationship may be compared with proposals which appeared first in Hugh Ferriss's *The Metropolis of Tomorrow* and then in Raymond Hood's *City of Skyscrapers*, as well as in the work of Eliel Saarinen, Le Corbusier, and the Japanese Metabolists. All these proposals treat the city/skyscraper as a volumetric syntax in which volume and mass remain impenetrable, divisions are abrupt, and transitions absent. While the totality of the skyscraper/city is equipped with bridges that unite the individual skyscrapers, there are no true transitions. The passages between one building and the next are strictly linear and abrupt, as relationships shift from point to point. In the case of Saarinen's magnificent project for the Chicago lakefront, this same principle emerges as a series of more subtle transitions.

On the other hand, the relationship that is established between the skyscraper in the city and between the skyscrapers and the city is symbolic rather than volumetric, a complex play of transitions which generate signifying networks that interact with the rest of the city.

It is no accident that Portman, Johnson, and Roche all use mirrors in their buildings; in each instance the mirror not only reveals the nature of the building but also its role as a condenser, as a place where codes intersect codes, and as a fragment of a larger text, the city. The dematerialization of the building through reflections establishes the structure as both itself and the other. It is a signifier whose meanings are given to it by other signifiers. The traditional meaning, the content, has been dissolved.

The Shaft

The shaft of the column having been transformed, fragmented, and stretched through a process of anamorphosis now becomes one with the base and the capital as in the case of the Seagram Building and the towers of Sixth Avenue, which are the purest expressions of that phenomenon. These buildings condense in different ways the role that was previously shared between each part. The building as

Crowding Towers. *Drawing by Hugh Ferriss, 1929.*

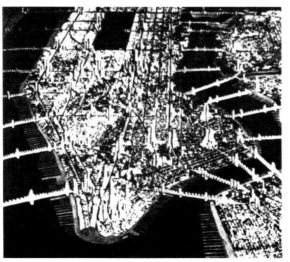

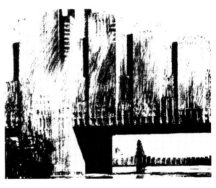

Manhattan 1950. Project by Raymond Hood.

Detail.

Apartments on Bridges. *Drawing by Hugh
Ferriss, 1929.*

Project for a lakefront for Chicago. Eliel Saarinen, 1923.

a whole is the symbol of its own power and acquires its meaning in a contextual relationship, that is, as a result of the difference between the "marked" and the "unmarked" elements which constitute the city.[15] The claim that modern form has been desemanticized is thus invalidated; these buildings take their meanings in relation to their context. Their symbolic functioning arises out of relationships of substitution and from an exchange of meanings: for symbolization is after all no more than exchange itself. The skyscraper, like all objects in a capitalistic society, has the property of incorporating within itself two values, those of use and those of exchange or aggregated value, thus giving rise to fetishism. Architecture is no exception to this rule, and the possibility of desemanticization is, therefore, a fantasy. The competition between skyscrapers is based on their exchange rather than on their use value, that is to say, on their attributes as the highest, the biggest, the strangest, the most beautiful, and so on.

Openings

If at first the termination of the skyscraper was necessary in order to transform the metaphor of "touching the clouds" into an apparent reality, in an age when this "touching" is literally possible by means of satellites and space voyages such symbolization is no longer required. Instead it is necessary to remember that it is from earth that space is approached and earth remains on center. The space between

Towers on Sixth Avenue. These towers, which are an extension of Rockefeller Center, are from right to left: Time Life, Celanese, McGraw-Hill, and Exxon.

World Trade Center and Manhattan by night.

Vertical Assembly Building, John F. Kennedy Space Center, Cape Kennedy. Urbahn, Roberts, Seeley & Moran, architects.

buildings, as it occurs in the World Trade Center, may be read as a metaphor for this "race" to outer space. Where the skyscraper used to race upward seeking its limit, this limit can now no longer be thought of in the same way. The opening itself between the buildings themselves appears as the signifier. The World Trade Center is only "detailed" for the level in which it emerges from the ground. The buildings themselves could be cut off at any point.

There is, however, a unique skyscraper, one which is "the biggest one in the world—four times the volume of the Empire State Building," according to the official guide. This is a structure for the assembly of an object that will materialize its own metaphor; it is the Assembly Building at Cape Kennedy whose lateral façade recalls the silhouette of the Empire State Building and whose double doors anticipate the World Trade Center. Here the skyscraper has unfolded and the metaphor of the skyscraper is realized in a building which as pure structure contains the "spire" that will literally reach to the sky. Here technology has been transformed by metonymy into pure symbol. The skyscraper is now a door, a door both to space and to the city, to the plurality of meaning.

Notes

1. Francisco Mujica, *History of the Skyscraper* (New York: Archeology and Architecture Press, 1930); Winston Weisman, "New York and the Problem of the First Skyscraper," *Journal of the Society of Architectural Historians*, 1953, Vol. XII, No. 1, and "A New View of Skyscraper History," *The Rise of an American Architecture*, Edgar Kaufmann, Jr., ed. (New York: Praeger Publishers, 1970); Carson Webster, "The Skyscraper, Logical and Historical Considerations," *Journal of the Society of Architectural Historians*, 1959, Vol. XVIII, No. 4; Claude Bragdon, "The Skyscraper," *Architectural Record*, December 1909; Montgomery Schuyler, "Skyscraper up to Date" (1899), "The Evolution of the Skyscraper" (1909), "The Towers of Manhattan and Notes of the Woolworth Building" (1913), *American Architecture and Other Writings*, William Jordy and Ralph Coe, eds. (Harvard, 1961); Alfred Bossom, *Building to the Skies, the Romance of the Skyscraper* (New York, 1934); William Jordy, *American Architecture and Urbanism*; Hugh Ferriss, *Metropolis of Tomorrow* (New York, 1929); Manfredo Tafuri, "La Montagna Disincantata. Il Grattacielo e la Città," *La città americana della guerra civile al "New Deal,"* Ciucci, Dal Co, Manieri, Elia, Tafuri, co-authors (Bari: Laterza, 1973); Walter Kilham, Jr., *Raymond Hood Architect, Form Through Function in the American Skyscraper* (New York: Architectural Book Publishers, 1973).

2. Weisman, "A New View of Skyscraper History," pp. 115–119. This study is interesting because it postulates a certain autonomy of the structure of meaning.

3. Mario Gandelsonas, "The Architectural Signifier/Column," paper presented at the First Congress of the International Association of Semiotics, Milan, June 1974.

4. The International Competition for a New Administration Building for the *Chicago Tribune*, Chicago, 1923.

5. Joseph Rykwert, *Adam's House in Paradise* (New York: Museum of Modern Art, 1972), p. 166.

6. Manfredo Tafuri, "La Montagna Disincantata. Il Grattacielo e la Città."

7. Ibid.

8. The skyscraper in this way places architecture in a crisis insofar as it indicates a direction whose signifying complexity is unequaled in the history of architecture.

9. In the development of the tower-type, there are cases wherein the column-scheme is reproduced such that the elements relate to each other in different ways: either the body is developed, as happens in Leroy Buffington's design of 1888 for a twenty-story building, or the base develops, taking the form of setbacks, as illustrated in Adler and Sullivan's scheme for the Odd Fellows Temple in 1891. The crest may develop as it does in the Spreckles Building, San Francisco, designed by J. W. and M. J. Reid in 1897; or the whole building may become a true column in its proportions as occurs in Magney and Tusler's Foshay Tower of 1927–1928. Although we are developing here the argument by speaking about crests either as capital or as fundamental element, there are other skyscrapers that do not possess them which, on the other hand, are complete parallelopipeds; for the most part, these cases enter that category just after the tripartite phase or else represent transformations of it.

10. Bossom, *Building to the Skies, the Romance of the Skyscraper*, p. 17.

11. Mario Gandelsonas, "World Trade Center" (unpublished essay, 1973).

12. The buildings on Sixth Avenue belong to such different corporations as Exxon, McGraw-Hill, and Celanese.

13. Walter McQuade, "A Daring New Generation of Skyscrapers," *Fortune*, Feb. 1973.

14. D. Agrest, "Design vs. Non-Designed Public Places," paper presented at the First Congress of the International Association of Semiotics, Milan, June 1974. Published as "Design versus Non-Design," *Oppositions* 6, 1976 and this volume.

15. Roland Barthes, "Semiologie et Urbanisme," *L'Architecture d'Aujourd'hui*, 153.

THE CITY AS THE PLACE OF REPRESENTATION

The soothsayers who found out from time what it had in store certainly did not experience time as either homogeneous or empty. Anyone who keeps this in mind will perhaps get an idea of how past times were experienced in remembrance—namely, in just the same way. We know that the Jews were prohibited from investigating the future. The Torah and the prayers instruct them in remembrance, however. This stripped the future of its magic, to which all those succumb who turn to the soothsayers for enlightenment. This does not imply, however, that for the Jews the future turned into homogeneous, empty time. For every second of time was the strait gate through which the Messiah might enter.   Walter Benjamin, *Thesis in the Philosophy of History*

The city has always occupied a privileged place in the architectural dream—it is the place where all orders are possible. It is the mythical place where myriad different orders are projected, an unlimited repository. But the city is also the concrete place of the accumulation of these orders, which are superimposed upon, annihilate, or support each other. The space of the myth is simultaneously the record of the myth, a presence and an absence, a reality and an abstraction. It is this struggle between the city's position as actual accumulation of conflicting orders—its orderlessness—and its desire for order that has characterized the development of theories about the city and architecture.

In his text "The Analytical Language of John Wilkins," Borges talks of a Chinese encyclopedia called *The Celestial Emporium of Benevolent Knowledge*, which divides animals into the following categories: "a) those that belong to the emperor, b) embalmed ones, c) those that are trained, d) suckling pigs, e) mermaids, f) fabulous ones, g) stray dogs, h) those that are included in this classification, i) those extremely agitated, j) innumerable, k) those drawn with a very fine camel's hair brush, l) et cetera, m) those that have just broken the flower vase, n) those that resemble flies from a distance."[1] As Michel Foucault indicates in *The Order of Things*, what is made impossible by this classification is not the vicinity of these things but the very place where they could be neighbors. The monstrosity of the enumeration lies in the fact that it leaves in ruins the common place where things might meet.[2] Borges removes the place where things could be juxtaposed (in terms of the famous surrealist image, it is the table on which the umbrella and the sewing machine were placed that is removed) "where, since the beginning of time, language and space have intersected."[3]

The disorder that results is not one of incongruence, the response not one of surprise at unlikely juxtapositions. Rather, the disorder that Borges describes is one that manifests the fragments of a great number of possible orders in a dimension without law or geometry—an unorderable, heteroclitic dimension.[4] Things are arranged in such a way that it is impossible to conceive of them as occupying a common place. Foucault writes:

Utopias *afford consolation: Although they have no real locality there is nevertheless a fantastic, untroubled region in which they are able to unfold; they open up cities with vast avenues, superbly planted gardens, countries where life is easy, even though the road to them is chimerical.* Heterotopias *are disturbing, probably because they secretly undermine language, because they make it impossible to name this* and *that, because they shatter or tangle common names, because they destroy "syntax" in advance, and not only the syntax with which we construct sentences but also that less apparent syntax which causes words and things (next to and also opposite one another) to "hold together." . . . Language is ruined, the common aspect of place and name has been lost.*[5]

To this distortion that makes classification itself unthinkable, to this table without a coherent space, Borges gives a name and an identity; it becomes a mythical land, a precise region representing for the West a great reservoir of utopias.[6]

This order of the unthinkable is manifested in Piranesi's Campo Marzio, constructed of a space literally in ruins. The past, the forbidden, the spatially and socially impossible, and that which is eliminated from space and excluded from society and culture are all synthesized in Piranesi's spaces, which were themselves unthinkable at the time of their production—spaces that present the city as both myth and object, ruinous spaces, heterotopias. The other extreme of architecture's mythical tradition is the utopia. The city has always been a fertile ground for utopias, perhaps in response to the need to overcome the anguish created by the heterotopic nature of the city itself.

The city can be described not only in spatial but also in temporal terms. The city exists through time, a dimension that is lived as the fantasy of the new and the fantasy of the past. The confrontation between the fantasy and the real appears as a characteristic feature in the consideration of the representation of the city. Piranesi and Le Corbusier represent two ways of confronting reality, in one case with the past, in the other with the future. Two forms of representation appear, the representation of the existing real and the representation of fantasy. The two forms of representing and confronting the fantasy with the existent city are based on the notion of destruction—the ruin in one instance, tabula rasa in the other: a vision of a new, impossible city with the ruin at its origin in the one case and in the other the destruction of the existing city. One is founded on remembering, the other on forgetting. Together they represent the beginning and the culmination of modernity. They are the crucial points from which to consider the city in relation to language, that is, in relation to the way in which the organization of space and language intersect in the city as the scene of the social production of meaning.

The distinction between the representation of the city and the city as representation becomes crucial in articulating this problem. It is from this point, the terrain on which the negative and positive utopias—two modes of the modern conception of language—contest, that we must proceed, backward and forward in time, through the city.

The Space of Representation

During the Renaissance, the method of understanding the world—knowledge—advances by establishing similarities between things, images, and words—in short, by establishing analogies. Analogy is the prevailing figure in the treatises on painting and architecture of the period: urban space, the space of perspectival painting, and the space of the theater are constructed and understood as analogues of one another. The macrocosm is analogous to the microcosm, the city to a set of houses, the house to a set of rooms.[7] One "knows" only the same. With the enormous change in the means of understanding the methodology of knowledge that occurs in the seventeenth century, analogy is replaced by attention to the relationship between things and their hidden meaning, between a sign and its concept. Representation and its theories and techniques assume a major role in every aspect of culture.[8]

This turning point in the representation of the city coincides precisely with the formation of the capital city. The city at this point is no longer viewed as the center of a state; its monuments are no longer symbolic centers of power, as was true of the Renaissance city. Instead the city becomes the center of a group of states, and the city as a whole is imbued with monumentality and assumes a role of representation. Aided by the many rhetorical devices developed in painting and the other arts, this city becomes a tool of persuasion. The familiar example of Rome illustrates this technique.[9]

Allegories and symbols are created to represent the hidden meanings of our terrestrial life. The city and architecture represent what cannot be seen—the secrets of the universe as understood by religion—thus becoming the means by which one is able to "see" the invisible. Allegory and other rhetorical figures serve to create effects of the real and the natural. The application of rhetorical devices to the arts was not, of course, new: what is new here is the use of these devices in the development of an urban discourse, of a representation of the city in its relation to other dominant discourses.

At the end of the seventeenth century, after the battles of the Reformation and in the face of its newly defined political and religious roles, the transformation of Rome became necessary. It is within this context that Pope Sixto V and Domenico Fontana presented a scheme for the development of the city. The great arteries proposed by Fontana are intended to link the great Christian basilicas in Rome to facilitate the circulation of the faithful. The sacred character of the city is no longer restricted to a special section. Instead the whole city becomes a sacred space, acquiring an ideological role. The streets connecting the churches soon become important commercial arteries; several goals are attained simultaneously as the religious or ideological, the economic, and the political advance along the same route. Catholicism, which comprises a collective, or social, religion as opposed to the individualism of Protestantism, constructs a new city—a city of streets and squares rather than of buildings.[10]

In this space the conception of the monument is transformed and becomes more urban. The work of Bernini, especially his restructuring of St. Peter's, provides the major example of such a conception. The monument is seen as persisting through

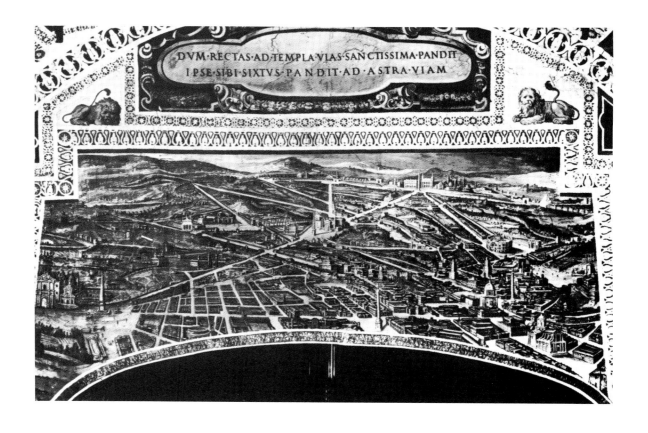

Plan of Rome of Sixto V, 1589.

Anonymous.

time, preserving its own ideological value. Argan provides a marvelous analysis of the transformations of St. Peter's by Maderno and later by Bernini.[11] When Maderno added the façade to the church, he profoundly changed the sense that Michelangelo had given the building. The dome, which had been the central element, becomes only a background element, placed on a secondary plane in relation to the façade. When Bernini later set out to design a portico, he conceived, after a prolonged analysis of various possible configurations, an elliptical colonnade. Clearly he intended to bracket Maderno's façade, to place it in a secondary position with respect to the monument's central, allegorical element, its dome. The elliptical portico diminishes the importance of the façade, which becomes merely diaphragmatic in relation to the dome.

A round portico would have placed the dome, the center of the façade, and the obelisk on a diameter. Bernini's elliptical portico, however, creates two crossed perspectival views that place the façade in parentheses, enclosing it in another space having its own value. Bernini also develops and strengthens the theme of the dome by repeating its paired columns in the form of the colonnade. These two strategies of bracketing and repetition produce a specific manifestation of monumentality. The monumental and allegorical roles, formerly concentrated in the dome, are allowed an egress by the giant portico and begin to pervade the urban realm. The monumental city, thus allegorized, establishes its permanence throughout history. Bernini's dome becomes, symbolically, the head of Christianity, and his portico is like two arms embracing all of humanity.[12]

The city is not only the representation but also the scene of power. The façades are not only the frontal place of a building but also surfaces defining a theatrical space, a theatrical space that loses its precision in this crossing of perspectives. This urban space, perceived in the Renaissance as an analogue of theatrical space, is now perceived as the manifest theater of hidden meanings. A theater of representation replaces a theater of analogy, and the techniques of and studies on perspective are employed in the production of space and not only in its representation.

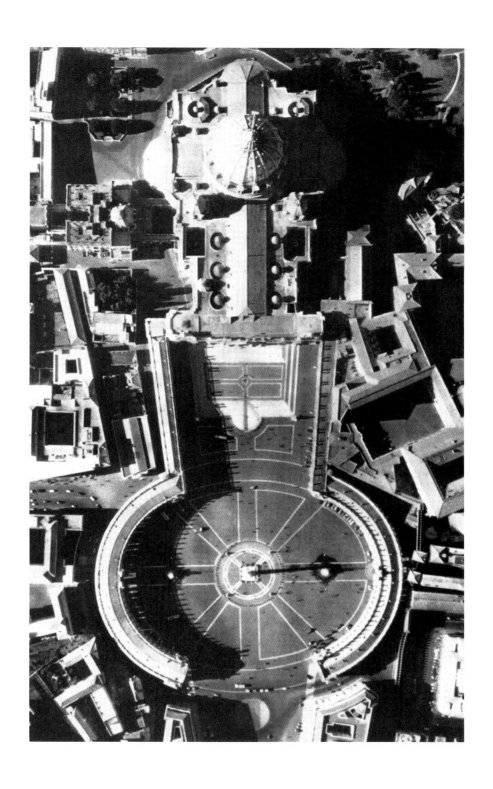

Aerial view of St. Peter's Square in Rome.

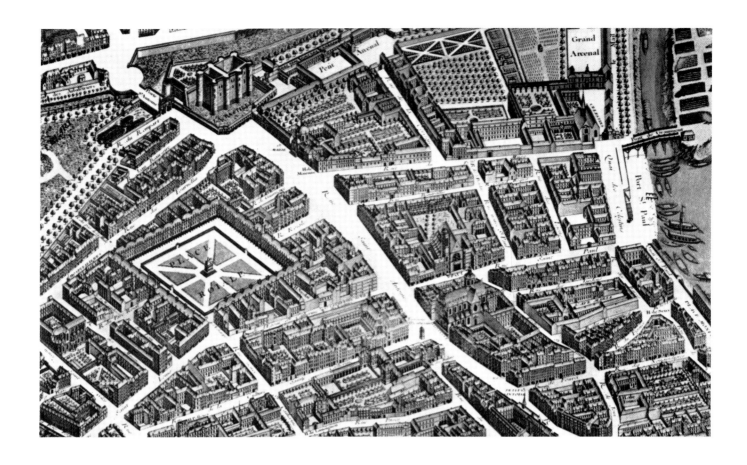

The Place of Social Action

With the establishment of an absolute monarchy, a gradually developing bourgeoisie, and the loss of faith in the self-evidence of the divine presence, the eighteenth century systematically turns toward a representation of space in which "place becomes event and space, emotion."[13] In the city—clearly exemplified in Paris—the square luxuriates in a waste. Places are consecrated to princes, saints, victories, and friendly nations. It has been said that the eighteenth century discovers pleasure as an object of reflection as well as an inflection of experience.[14] The relationship shifts between pleasure and virtue. No longer does pleasure await the authorization of a moral judgment but is aligned positively with sensibility. "The conflict between judgment and sensibility is reconciled in a theory of complex beauty, order, and variation."[15] No longer is pleasure viewed as the residue of an escaping power but rather as a fundamental reservoir of energy from which a totally new social order could be built—pleasure becomes the despair of the faltering aristocracy and the hope of the rising bourgeoisie.[16]

Plan of Paris by Turgot—Place Royale and the Bastille.

Images are made representing pleasure that words forbid. A whole ideology of fiction is mobilized to support a theatricality that comes increasingly to pervade and

Louis Paret, Masqued Ball, *1766. Prado Museum, Madrid.*

City Hall and L'Hémicycle de la Carrière at Nancy by Germain Boffrand, 1715.

Perspective view of the lighting of the Rue de la Ferronnerie, 1739. Design by Charles-Nicholas Cochin, engraved by J. de Seve. Geneva—Bibliotèque Publique et Universitaire.

Commemoration of the taking of the Bastille at the Champ-de-Mars, July 14, 1792 by Jean-Louis Prieur.

inflect various aspects of cultural life. Rhetoric displaces objects, or the lack of objects, in images of other things—"masks whose intention is to unmask." Art becomes a vehicle of pleasure, eliciting pleasure from its spectators and making it its subject matter. The boundaries dividing theatrical spectacle from quotidian ceremony collapse.[17]

"From the *fêtes galantes* of the *fêtes de la Révolution* the century's transformation of its multiple ceremonies of pleasure can be traced." Within a social group dedicated to the pursuit of pleasure, the fête appears as "the dispensation par excellence of a life of dispensation"; it is also "the instant par excellence in a life of successive instants." The fête pays tribute to the nature of a pleasure that ceaselessly renews each fading moment.[18]

But behind the fêtes, always, is the continuity of social life. Critics seek an understanding of the fête that would also acknowledge the perdurability of this realm and a concept of the fête no longer as exclusive but including a whole people—a fête that would break down social barriers. The spatial organization of theaters, with sequences of individual balconies separating small groups from one another, clearly serves and perpetuates a notion of pleasure as private. Such organization is decidedly opposed to Rousseau's vision of the fête as an assembly of people collectively sharing freedom. The presence of the people is enough to create a global event where spectators and spectacle are one and the same. Desire is sublimated and directed toward constructing a popular unity.[19]

In this process is a tendency toward the elimination of art as representation. The city is the scene of the spectacle, rather than the representation of theatrical space. The revolutionary fêtes are the culmination of the city's presentation of itself as a social discourse.[20] By this discursive ordering, theatrical space is rendered temporal, becoming the instance of a historical intersection. It is during this period, according to Hegel, that great artistic production shifts from the visual arts to the fields of music and poetry.[21] While in the sixteenth and seventeenth centuries representation has to do with rhetoric, with the development of a grammar or articulation—especially as developed by the Grammaire de Port Royale—representation is now arranged according to sequential series.[22] It is at this moment that narrative increases in importance, transforming static space into a sequence. By this means an appropriation of space occurs. The narrativized city becomes the place of a scene, the site of a struggle, and is read and rewritten by the scriptings of a narrative.

The transformation of the Renaissance city's theatrical space from an empty physical scene to one of action marks a trajectory of change in the representation of power from the scene of the possessors to that of the dispossessed, from delimitation to occupation of space. Architecture is on one side and social discourse on the other. And in this split lies the seed for the very "death" of architecture itself.

The City as Language

The changes just described are consonant with changes occurring in theories of language. As the issue of language becomes primarily one of signification, theories of art shift attention from representation to production. Lessing's *Laocoon* is a landmark in this shift, breaking radically from the prevailing theories of the relationship between painting and poetry.[23] According to previous theories, a great poem could inspire a great painting, and a painting could represent a poetic text. Lessing, however, distinguishes painting's spatiality from poetry's temporality. He ascribes to each a specificity of laws and meanings; painting and poetry signify differently and do not represent similar, preexisting contents. For each there are subject matters proper to its particular means of signification.

Lessing's distinction generates dispute between rationalist and naturalist theories of representation. Those who, like Laugier and Milizia, see the city as a representation of nature find themselves contradicting their belief in order and reason. Milizia's dictum that whoever could draw a garden could also design a city becomes problematic. It is now clear that naturalist ideology, which employed perspective not as an element of production but as one of verification, confounded the *veduttisti* with the architect.[24]

As a consequence of this late eighteenth-century negation of representation, the task of the visual arts can no longer be seen as the simple fixing of an image. Instead these arts come to signify their own action, or their own absence.[25] The problem thus posed to the visual arts—arts after all of presence—of expressing their own negation, their absence, is solved, historically, by a preoccupation with

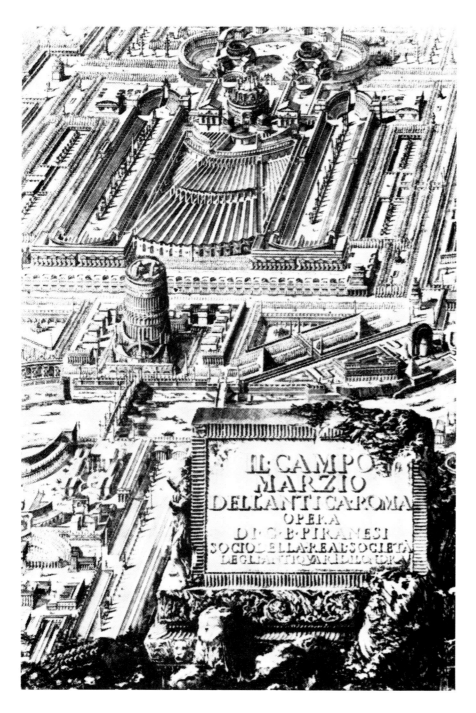

Campo Marzio by Giovanni Battista Piranesi. Perspective view of Hadrian's Tower, the crypt entrance, and the two adjacent stadia.

Ruines 1780? Giovanni Niccolò Servandoni.

objects whose presence speaks of what is no longer there: ruins. Ruins are the favorite subject matter of the *veduta* and landscapes. Piranesi is boldly emblematic of this concern. Appearing initially to reconcile, in his Campo Martio, theories of the natural as realized by the artificial by an exasperating typological series, Piranesi can be seen in fact to condemn his own present without seeking shelter in a tranquilizing future.[26] At the same time he makes evident the changes architecture had undergone at the level of language and the impossibility of its representing anything beyond itself. His Carceri, in which he represents the forbidden and the perverse, are conceived in dramatic opposition to the humanistic, analogical mode, which was based on a perpetual return of the same. Piranesi, by underscoring the specificity of architectural practice, gestures toward that which is different, the "other," which was never seen.

Yet this order of the invisible is radically different from Bernini's. The Carceri do not represent a world lying behind the social, behind meaning, but one that is excluded from society and sense, at the same time as it is reappropriated by them and preserved as foreign. Cryptic inscriptions on the fireplaces make reference to hidden occult texts. The ruins reveal/hide a mystery, a life that once was but that will never again be known. Piranesi here opens the way for a modern reading of the city and architecture by which what is considered is not the meaning inherent in buildings but the way they enter into relational structures to produce it.[27]

From this point on, architecture could be studied like language, as an autonomous structure. The focus shifts to the syntactic relationship between basic architectural elements independent of any representational function. This shift is evident in Durand's typological classification of buildings. Urban buildings exhibit styles that adopt the role of representation independent of typologies, in a city that seems to become a classifying device. This is especially apparent in the development of the project for the Ringstrasse in Vienna—a Beaux-Arts precursor of modern town planning.

The Temporal Dimension: Diachronic and Synchronic Axes

The city, whose peculiar nature it is to superimpose its diachronic and synchronic axes, is a presence in perpetual oscillation between past and present. Its past is its concrete, built forms, juxtapositions and superimpositions of so many already

Carcere, with a large number of human and sculpted figures, second state.

Carcere, with numerous wooden galleries and a drawbridge, second state.

past futures. Its future is a projected, homogeneous, and empty time outside of history, an abstraction, an order suspended in a universal time and place. It is this imbrication of temporal and spatial axes that is at issue in the modern conception of the city, which makes any merely formal discourse on the city inadequate and requires a consideration of social production.

This recalls our discussion of Piranesi and Le Corbusier as extreme examples of the way in which the city's temporal dimension tends to produce negative or positive utopias. Piranesi's obsessive envisioning of the past and Le Corbusier's equally obsessive vision of the future perform acts of violence on the city—Piranesi through a wild proliferation of types, Le Corbusier through a belief in the ultimate omnipotence of prototype. Both develop readings of the contemporary city, but where one reads in it the ruins of the past and projects an impossible future, the other sees the objects that make the economy the machinery of industry and of the state and projects a possible future. One presents a negative, the other a positive, utopia. The typological game creates a city of monuments in an impossible typological space that will only be realized in a modern concept of space and in the architecture of the American city.

Piranesi and Le Corbusier mark the beginning and the development of modernity. In a telescopic vision toward the past Piranesi flattens time in a synchronic vision of history while Le Corbusier flattens time, homogenizing it in a vision toward the future, thus producing a complete synchrony. Both heterotopia (or negative utopia) and utopia speak about time while denying history. Piranesi makes explicit the mechanisms of architecture as an autonomous language, and Le Corbusier invokes a referent that has no actual existence. Both thereby deny history and the operations of representation. Together the work of these two architects constitutes a point from which the vicissitudes of the modern city may be understood in relation to the problem of representation. They represent the historical moment from which one may look back to the seventeenth-century capital city's concern with representation as the focus of forms of knowledge and from which one may look forward to the twentieth-century monopolistic city's decidedly antirepresentational stance.

The City and Antirepresentation

The poles of debate, Piranesi's critical skepticism and Le Corbusier's positivism, are in evidence, either successively or simultaneously, throughout the history of architecture. But nowhere are they more clearly defined than in discourses on the city. Perhaps this is because the city is the arena of architectural discourse. To think of the city is to think of architecture, for the city is the limit of architecture. It is its unconscious, the place of intersection of social forces with language.[28]

It is with modern urbanism as a discipline that architecture finally directs the discourse of the city, a discourse marked by the dichotomy between form and function and by a need to reinvent a vocabulary for a language that no longer has a lexicon. This discourse thus develops in a relatively autonomous manner. Architecture, which had always been seen primarily through the city, begins to make the city its object of institutionalized, professional study. Le Corbusier appears as a clear example of this new condition. While the relationship between the discourses of the city and of architecture was always a possibility, it had always been accomplished through the intermediation of a third representational discourse (e.g., painting, linguistics). For the first time the discourse of architecture and that of urbanism engage in an immediate relationship, brought together over a common concern—the city.

Complications arise, however, over the fact that the urban discourse (or the planning discourse into which it had been transformed) is at the same time the mediating discourse between the dominant social and architectural ideologies. The conjunction is highly problematic. Architectural discourse, which had previously been structured around the opposition of sensation and reason, particularly as it gave rise to the opposition of form and function, art and technique, encounters the urban discourse at a moment when it has been transformed into a specific planning discourse. And whereas Renaissance architecture had represented a text that was clearly external to it, modern architecture now represents a discourse—planning—that is apparently internal but actually external. Architecture thus loses all distance from this discourse, merges completely with it, and is finally, for reasons I will make clear, thrown into crisis by it.

The planning discourse, which had developed in tandem with the dominant ideology of the social sciences and systems theory, was constructed on a communications model, a model that concentrates on the transmission of information and the transportability of meaning to the exclusion of signification. Thus, in its encounter with the city, it develops and elaborates the functional pole of architecture's form/function dichotomy. According to this model, urban chaos is a new kind of order. Space and physical place are no longer necessary; a "nonurban realm" was advocated in which accessibility rather than proximity is at issue.[29] The only order left to the city is that which could be represented by computer diagrams or the alienated vision of the television set. The only work left for architects influenced in turn by planning ideology is the designing of more efficient activities systems. Architecture, in short, has been cut off from its own specific knowledge, its own power to intervene. The city has destroyed not only its own configuration but also, and more important, architecture itself. If the discourse of urbanism has brought architecture in its relation to the city to this dead end, it is due in part to the classical residue of representation still at play in its functionalist conception.

Paradoxically, architecture must turn once again to the city—this time to rescue it from the crisis into which the city itself has forced it. If the dichotomy between formalist and economic discourses, together with a denial of history, has led to such a crisis, new life will come neither from merely reviving and reversing this same dichotomy nor from mechanically and equally ahistorically reviving past forms, but from fundamentally changing the understanding of the city as an object of study.

Notes

1. Jorge Luis Borges, "The Analytical Language of John Wilkins," in *Other Inquisitions*, trans. Ruth C. L. Simms (New York: Simon and Schuster, 1965), p. 103.

2. Michel Foucault, *The Order of Things: An Archaeology of the Human Sciences* (New York: Random House, 1973), p. xvi.

3. Ibid., p. xvii.

4. Ibid.

5. Ibid., p. xviii.

6. Ibid.

7. Erwin Panofsky, *Meaning in the Visual Arts* (Garden City, N.Y.: Doubleday, 1955). Also see *Studies in Iconology* (Oxford: Oxford University Press, 1939) and Guilio Carlo Argan, *Renaissance Painting* (New York: Dell, 1967).

8. Foucault, *The Order of Things*.

9. Sigfried Giedion, *Space, Time, and Architecture* (Cambridge, Mass.: MIT Press, 1941); Heinrich Wolflin, *Renaissance and Baroque* (Ithaca, N.Y.: Cornell University Press, 1966); G. C. Argan, *L'Architettura barroca in Italia aldo* (Milan: Garzanti, 1957) and *L'Europe des capitales, 1600–1700* (Paris: Skira, 1964).

10. Argan, *L'Architettura barroca in Italia*; Giedion, *Space, Time, and Architecture*.

11. Rudolph Wittkower, *La cupola di San Pietro di Michelangelo* (Florence, 1964). Also see Argan, *L'Europe des capitales* and *L'Architettura barroca in Italia*.

12. Argan, *L'Europe des capitales* and *L'Architettura barroca in Italia*.

13. Jean Starobinski, *L'Invention de la liberté* (Paris: Skira, 1964), p. 17.

14. Ibid., p. 43.

15. Ibid., p. 53.

16. Ibid., p. 54.

17. Ibid., p. 64.

18. Ibid., p. 85.

19. Ibid., p. 100.

20. Ibid., p. 102.

21. Ibid., p. 102; J. J. Rousseau, *Essai sur l'origine des langues* (Geneva, 1781); Diderot, *Paradoxe sur le commedien* (Paris: Flammarion, 1967); Mona Ozouf, *La fête révolutionnaire, 1789–1799* (Paris: Gallimard, 1976).

22. Foucault, *The Order of Things*.

23. G. E. Lessing, *Laocoon, Des frontières de la peinture et de la poésie* (Paris: Hermann, 1964 [1766]). See also the introduction by J. Bialostocka.

24. Marc Antoine Laugier, *Essai sur l'architecture* (Paris, 1753), English translation, *An Essay on Architecture by M. A. Laugier*, trans. and intro. Wolfgang and Anni Hermann (Los Angeles: Hennessey and Ingalls, 1977).

25. Starobinski, *L'Invention de la liberté*.

26. Manfredo Tafuri, *Giovanni Battista Piranesi: L'Architettura come utopia negativa* (Turin: Torino Accademia delle Scienze, 1972); John Harris, "Le Geay, Piranesi, and International Neo-Classicism in Rome 1740–1750," *Essays in the History of Architecture Presented to Rudolph Wittkower* (London: Phaidon, 1969); G. B. Piranesi, *Prima Parte di Architetture e Prospettive* (Rome, 1743).

27. Tafuri, *Piranesi*.

28. This is elaborated in "Design versus Non-Design," this volume; see also Le Corbusier, *Urbanisme* (Collection de l'esprit nouveau, 1924, Freal, 1966).

29. Representative of this tendency are: Richard Meier, *A Communications Theory of Urban Growth* (Cambridge, Mass.: MIT Press, 1962); Brian McLoughlin, *Urban and Regional Planning: A Systems Approach* (London: Faber and Faber, 1969); Jay Forrester, *Urban Dynamics* (Cambridge, Mass.: MIT Press, 1969); Melvin Webber, "The Urban Place and the Non-place Urban Realm," *Explorations into Urban Structure* (Philadelphia: University of Pennsylvania Press, 1964). For a criticism of these works, see "The Misfortunes of Theory," this volume.

Atlantic City and *Superman II* are films that develop around cities. Adventures of a hero, private drama of an antihero; one fantastic and the other realist. It is not the artistic qualities of these films as such that make them worthy of criticism, but rather the potential they provide for reflection on the relationship between film and architecture. Looking at these two films, one inevitably thinks about architecture in relation to cinema, for architecture has a central role in both films.

The relationship between architecture and film has a long history, though one that has not been acknowledged or made explicit. Of course, I am talking here about the modernist tradition that corresponds to the development of cinema. From the point of view of film production, architecture is an almost unavoidable element of film. It ranges from being a mere background against which action takes place, without particular care for or emphasis on the architectural (spatial, formal, and symbolic) features or qualities of that background, to the other extreme, where architecture is almost the inspiring force behind the film. Fritz Lang's *Metropolis* is a rather obvious example of the latter. If instead we adopt the vantage point of architecture, it seems as though film has never been considered a driving force or influence behind architectural production or theory.

Architecture traditionally has been related to painting and sculpture, those permanent visual testimonies of culture. This has been particularly true since the Renaissance. Together with painting, architecture has been linked to theater in relation to the discovery of perspective and the definition of the theatrical perspective of space.

During the first decades of this century, when architectural and urban theories with their corresponding images were developed, the art system that served as a reference was still painting—a two-dimensional reality, an abstraction. Despite the fact that film was being developed at the time with extraordinary vigor, it was not acknowledged in architecture. Today there is a renewed and different interest in the formal structures of the city and in its structures of meaning, whether as subjects of design (urban design) or as sources of inspiration for architectural form through notions such as typology, analogy, and reading. Given the nature of the problems facing architecture today and the characteristics of the city itself, it would seem that film is the most pertinent visual art to which architecture can relate. If this is the case, then the implications of the relationship between film and architecture are more complex than the usual assumption that architecture is merely a background or formal support for a film's content. Architectural form relates now to the form of film as one text to another, in terms of a structure composed of so many languages—or rather, fragments of languages—organized in time and through space. Film, analogous to the city, is a continuous sequence of spaces perceived through time. When the city is the subject matter of architecture and also of film, as is the case in these two films, one discovers a rather revealing situation.

The adventures of Superman, fallen to earth and now worthy of his name, begin in a metropolis known to mortals as Manhattan. The hero's unbelievable tasks take him from the core of Manhattan, Grand Central Station, to the core of another great city, the Eiffel Tower in Paris, before his return to Niagara Falls. There his heroic actions are interrupted temporarily for the sake of a sentimental life that cannot be, for psychology is not in the nature of this supernatural character (we find that love—or is it women—and power are contradictory terms). After an interlude in a crystal pied-à-terre at the North Pole, Superman moves out of ARKI-TEKTUR and back to the city to fight evil again on top of skyscrapers. There is no continuous drama here, just variations on the theme of good and evil in a series of situations and actions of sensationalist nature, evolving from the stone to the printed word. The city is the magnificent, fantastic set where everything is possible and where the unexpected can happen in the most familiar places with an irrefutable realism. The whole movie is only a fragment of a series of adventures that could continue endlessly; one can therefore interpret its aesthetic structures independently of its plot.

Atlantic City, on the other hand, is a drama played out among the ruins of the past life of an individual and of a city. That individual inhabits a literal ruin, where the debris of times past can be found. Scenes take place in various interiors that are linked by the boardwalk, the only remaining element of the city—as though the boardwalk itself constituted the city. Atlantic City interferes with and determines the destinies of the characters. The main characters remain there because they represent the myths of Atlantic City, myths that have broken down and have never been reconstructed. The dynamited hotel and demolished housing are testimonies to, more than symbols of, this process. The only thing that persists and remains is the boardwalk, which is also the site of the final scene.

Narrative is an essential element in the relationship between film and architecture. The stories represented in these films should not be seen only as content, for narrative is the essence of film form. The two forms of narrative structure are the epic and the dramatic. In his 1797 essay "On Epic and Dramatic Poetry," Goethe says that "the epic poem preferably describes man as he acts outwardly: battles, travels, and the kind of enterprise that requires some sensuous breadth; tragedy shows man led toward the inside, therefore the plot of a tragedy requires little space." This distinction is for Goethe equivalent to that between an action told in the form of a poem or novel (epic) and one performed on stage (dramatic). As elaborated by Arnheim, this distinction suitably applies to that between film and theater. The broad descriptions of diverse settings and actions that are typically epic hardly suit the space of the stage. Film has been able to take the epic to the stage; this is a major characteristic of the film medium.

There is still a distinction to be made within film between dramatic and epic film. Dramatic film, like drama, presents a problem and develops it as a dynamic, step-by-step plot until it reaches some form of solution. In epic film, on the other hand, a problem is neither analyzed nor solved. One permanent and constant problem is shown in a sequence of examples that do not represent steps toward its solution. The story merely ends at some point, or rather does not continue. Epic is static; it insists on the unchangeable nature of human beings.

The epic style of narration is a chainlike composition of episodes strung in sequences. This distinction between epic and dramatic serves to define the two different kinds of space and structure in *Superman II* and *Atlantic City* in relation to the city and architecture. The characteristics of epic and dramatic structures correspond perfectly to the mode of articulation of the form and meaning of architecture on the one hand and film on the other. These films are particularly revealing in this sense, for they are structured around two cities as different as New York and Atlantic City. It is not difficult to see how the city relates to an epic structure, whereas architecture corresponds to drama—not only in its structural characteristics but also in its traditional relationship with theater and dramatic space. Where the city, which is the place of representation, is the subject matter of the film, which is a mode of representation, form and content seem to coincide. Film and city rely on the same structural elements to give them meaning.

Superman represents the epic structure perfectly, and it does so through the city, or cities. It is built around an epic reading of the city that has no beginning or end, only a series of sequences through space based on the theme of good and evil.

Presented in its epic structure, the city is a major protagonist, and one is provided with a number of extraordinary readings of it through Superman's fantastic interaction with the city. If the film's epic structure makes it static, architecture is instead reversed and becomes—through the incorporation of the body in action—the most dynamic element of the film.

The city has always occupied a privileged place in visions of architecture; it is the mythical place where all orders are possible. In *Superman II* the city is both the mythical place of all possible orders and the concrete place of the accumulation of these orders. These sequences touch on the unconscious aspects of architecture; the physical reading of the city reveals dimensions that are usually repressed, such as the relationship between the body and architecture. Flying up through the Eiffel Tower from within, walking along the edge of Niagara Falls, and flying through the canyons formed by rows of skyscrapers all exacerbate the sensation of vertigo that architecture tries to counteract.

But if an epic reading of the city is possible in this film, also a very clear opposition between city and architecture can be perceived. Superman's dwelling presents a

Scene from Superman II. *Superman flying through New York City at Times Square.*

Superman flying through New York City, with the Brooklyn Bridge in the background.

*Superman on top of a highrise building in
Manhattan, with park-edge skyscrapers in
the background.*

*Superman in his ice dwelling at the North
Pole.*

Superman flying over New York City.

very different reality, an expressionist image in opposition to the realism of New York City or Niagara Falls. A paradoxical situation: where the architecture is presented as fantastic, all its expressionist kitsch (a symbol of modernity) is less fantastic than the realistic images in the fantastic reading of the city.

The fantastic cinema is possible because of the irrefutable realism of the photographic image and the new obsession with special effects. What appeals to people in fantastic cinematography is evidently its realism, the objectivity of the photographic image and the aura of incredibility surrounding each event. Through the realist approach the epic and the fantastic come together in *Superman II*: the epic as space and structure is possible through the realism of the fantastic. It is in this drama that the city has the starring role.

Realism seems to be more fantastic in the displaced elements that appear with the extraordinary power of the realistic image. The representation of the complexity of cultural codes taken for granted—such as the scenes where the kryptonites penetrate through walls and roofs, ignorant of such simple elements as doors—further emphasizes this effect. If realism appears in places such as cities and expressionism appears in a dwelling, it is not by chance, for in the first case we are confronted with a montage of objects and spaces, whereas the house is a single object and therefore constitutes a matter of style, a fetishistic object. Style and myth, the myth of modernity (the glass house), and the reality of modernity (the city) are here face to face. The remnant of visionary ideology in the expressionist image—a purely sculptural object devoid of context—makes it clear that only at the North Pole could one find such conditions, anachronistic compared to the richness of the city. Such imagery is of great vulnerability when vulgarized, becoming instant kitsch. On the other hand, it is impossible to transform the city into kitsch, for it is beyond style.

Although dealing with a city, *Atlantic City* exploits the type of structure that corresponds to drama, to theater: the boardwalk in Atlantic City is the backdrop against which the drama of lives and the drama of architecture are played. In *Atlantic City* the city exists through time, a dimension that is lived as the fantasy of the new and the fantasy of the past. The confrontation between fantasy and the real is characteristic of representations of the city. This aspect, so clearly manifest in this film, thus touches on the history of architecture and urban theories. The confrontation of the fantasy with the existent city, and the representation of both, is in these two films based on the notion of destruction. The visionary and the fantastic seem to go hand in hand with the notion of ruin. Negative and positive utopias coexist in these films as they do in our confrontation with the overpowering reality of the city.

Atlantic City reveals the opposition between the architect and the city and the architect's dream of changing the city by changing its architecture. The precepts of modern urbanism are shown here through destruction and replacement based solely on economic speculation.

Scene from Atlantic City.

The boardwalk is a theatrical space very much like the street, which occupied a major role in the theatrical space of the Renaissance. But, as opposed to the perspectives of *da Bibbiena* or Palladio's *Teatro Olimpico*, there is no perspective or sense of defined space here. The structure of the place and its role are theatrical without the attributes of theater; its meaning is impoverished by its reliance on outside meanings for its cultural survival.

It is in this that a major opposition exists between the relation of the city to the narrative structures of these two films. In *Superman II* the film's structure is epic, as is the formal structure of the city—an open-ended sequence of events as transformations of a constant theme. In *Atlantic City* the structure of the film is dramatic, theatrical but supported by a discordant spatial structure. This would hold true for other similar conditions, such as the strip.

Scene from Atlantic City.

The kind of realism in *Atlantic City* is not fantastic but relates to the dramatic structure of the space in the film in another way. There is no symbolism: the objects and actions are just signs describing the conditions of the drama. They do not correspond symbolically to the lives of the characters, and this disturbing displacement strengthens the effect of realism.

If the issue of realism appears, it is certainly as expression of a period dominated by the aesthetic of verisimilitude. But it is particularly relevant in dealing with the city, which is built up of so many verisimilitudes, where past and present coexist. One of the problems of modern urbanism has been its denial of the inevitable realistic presence in order to emphasize the aesthetic of abstraction, or rather of abstract form.

We have seen in this brief review the strong relationships between film and urban form. I said that in the beginning, modern urbanism related to painting and not to film. After more than sixty years this still seems to be true. It is to painting—whether collage or metaphysical—that the city as object of design is still related. This relationship between the city and painting is a legacy of the classical tradition of looking at the city from the point of view of architecture.

Looking at architecture from the point of view of the city would break with that tradition and instead articulate its relationship with the visual art that developed alongside the modern city: film.

What is there in mirrored glass that makes it so different from every other material in architecture? To start with a description of the material quality of a building is not the usual way of approaching an architectural problem. We do not speak of an architecture of stone, an architecture of brick, or an architecture of wood in order to explain a cultural phenomenon; why then do we qualify this architecture of mirrors by its materiality? Because buildings in materials such as these are the materialization of a previously drawn image. The mirror, however, *dematerializes* the building, producing other images instead.

The architecture of mirrors makes manifest the image as a conflicting element in architecture. More than anything else, mirror *is* image; it is the foremost vehicle not only for producing an image, but making that image manifest. From Narcissus's image reflected on the water to the catoptric machines of the seventeenth century, anything that deals specifically with the mirror deals with the question of image. In a more sophisticated elaboration, the mirror relates to our capacity to symbolize, as we face our own reflections, from the first time we contemplate our image in the mirror state (as developed by Lacan).[1] The relationship, then, between image and language, and our capacity for symbolization, inextricably tied to the imaginary "unification" of the fragmented body in "mirror stage," is at the heart of this discussion of the architecture of mirrors.

S. Freud's study at Bergasse 19, Vienna.
Photo by Edmund Engelman.

I will focus primarily on the relationship between image and language in architecture. In classical architecture, image and language were part of the same system;

the image was produced by the elements of architectural language and was put into a system with other architectural elements. The use of mirrors seems to have been a way of articulating specific architectural codes with other non-architectural codes, of dealing with images and modes of representation such as perspective and theater. In modern architecture, however, there is a split between image (in the classical sense) and language, or between representation and signification. In modern architecture, and particularly in the recent examples of mirrored architecture, the mirror is not in a system with architectural language or elements of language; instead, the image is articulated with other systems that focus on the image, such as photography and cinema. The meaning of an architecture of mirrors today is more a symptom of a moment of transition and adjustment than an established condition in and of itself.

The best example of the play between image and language in classical architecture is offered by Quatremère de Quincy in his book *De l'imitation*. In it he differentiates between imitation in the Beaux-Arts and imitation in nature. The latter is what he calls similitude by identical repetition, as opposed to the notion of imitation in the Beaux-Arts; to imitate in the Beaux-Arts is to produce the resemblance of one thing in another, which then becomes its image. The resemblance produced by imitation does not repeat the object in reality, but rather the object in image. Referring to the production of such an image, Quatremère talks about metaphoric operations and the elements of architecture in an almost linguistic manner. The notion of image seems to be essential to architecture; it is an object and not a mental construct; it is an object related to other objects (models) through elements of architectural languages.[2]

The mirror as used in classical interiors, from the seventeenth through the nineteenth centuries, was always part of the system of openings. To produce an image of imitation with an interior space, the mirror (not its image) was used as one of the elements of the architectural language, as one of the windows.[3] It was used to produce a dematerialization of the wall, creating visual illusions such as those of the Galerie des Glaces in Versailles by Jules Hardouin Mansart and Charles Le Brun in 1678. The image in the mirror, on the other hand, refers to architectural space, creating opening effects through perspective, depth, and rhythm, as may be seen in the oval room at the Hôtel de Soubise by Boffrand (1730). The value of the

Hôtel de Soubise, Salon Ovale. Germain Boffrand, with paintings by Charles Natoire, 1735.

Galerie des Glaces, Versailles. J. H. Mansart and Charles le Brun, c. 1678.

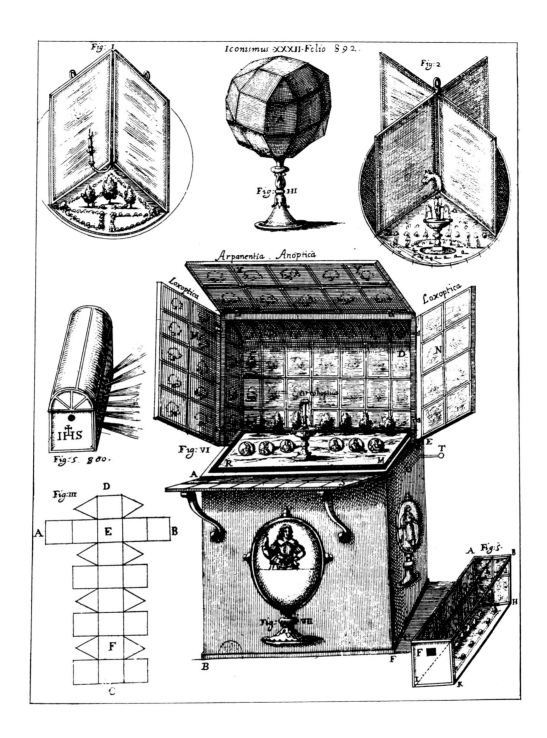

Catoptric Machines.

architectural space created by the image in the mirror opposed that of the pictorial space produced by the painted images on the ceiling, which are framed in a manner and position similar to the mirrors, as is exemplified clearly in The Mirror Room in the Residenzschloss at Fulda, Germany, by Adalbert von Walderdorff, Prince Bishop of Fulda in 1757, or in the Palazzo dell'Accademia Filarmonica in Turin (1760–70) by Benedetto Allieri and Giovanni Battista Borra.

The mirror, essentially an element of interior architecture and space, also addresses the question of representation; the mirror is a virtual plane between the real and the representation of the real. Because it has this property, it is also capable of playing with or tricking reality.

In the classical period, mirrors were used mostly in interiors and were consistently articulated with a spatial exploration that was occurring not only in architecture, where it was used to try to produce the dematerialization of the limits of the building through depth, light, and dynamic forms, but in other fields as well, such as painting and theater. Mirrors played a major role not only in the production of spatial effects, but in the articulation between theater and architecture. Catoptric machines of the seventeenth century, which were instrumental in the development of spatial illusions, attest to this. They dealt with questions of the perception of space and real space. These machines combined optical games with a knowledge of the laws and mechanisms of sight.[4]

Gaspar Schott, in his *Magia universalis naturae et artis* (1657), describes two catoptric mechanisms: Theatrical Machines with flat mirrors and Metamorphic Apparatus with curved and flat mirrors. The simplest combination consists of two flat mirrors articulated by a hinge over a disc, with variable angles. This elementary system is multiplied in the Catoptric Polydicticum Theater. It becomes a cabinet whose interior is covered with flat mirrors. "By the overload of shiny surfaces, by the richness and extravagance of its figurations, the Theatrum Polydicticum joins the scenography of the baroque."[5]

The same principle is later developed as a room, 6.5m × 3.5m, in which the players are no longer marionettes but human beings. Reconstructed at an architectural scale, the catoptric box now encloses a piece of life. Mirrors become bigger and are used prolifically; in keeping with a new visionary order, mural surfaces are

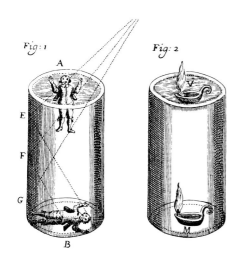

Cylindrical Mirror, Generator of Ghosts.

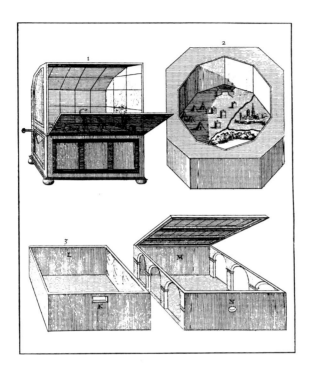 

Catoptric Boxes and Furniture.

Pommersfelden, the Mirror Cabinet, ceiling stucco by Daniel Schenk, c. 1715.

progressively broken and spaces become part of the world of illusion, as in the Maison-Lafitte Galerie des Glaces of 1650, the Salon de Guerre at Versailles of 1680, Bavarian baroque and rococo castles, and the Galleria degli Specchi at Mantova of the eighteenth century. Mirror-turning machines were also produced and were used to animate religious scenes. In the Speculum Polydictum of Jean Trithème (1518), eight different metamorphoses are proposed by the use of various combinations of mirrors and reflection mechanisms. In all these machines there is the suppression of all limits of space, which opens the way to all kinds of evasions.[6] At the center of this theater of pleasure or guilt is the subject: duplicated, repeated, metamorphosed, or suspended, in an indefinite space.

Hotel d'Uzes salon. Claude Nicolas Ledoux, 1769.

Mirror Salon of the Amelienburg. Johann Baptist Zimmerman, c. 1735.

The world of magic and miracles of the seventeenth and eighteenth centuries, where the inexplicable soul and the mysteries of life were justified through mystical and metaphysical constructs with the help of devices such as mirrors and catoptric machines, has its counterpart in the late nineteenth century: the development of psychoanalysis.

With the development of modern architecture, several very important changes occur. On one hand the perception of image becomes part of a whole different system of thought: no longer is an object related to the problem of representation or imitation; it becomes a mental construct. Historical discourse is replaced as a source of inspiration by the mechanisms of the mind, that is, the mechanisms of the unconscious, described by a psychological or a psychoanalytical discourse. On the other hand, the negation of the classical language of architecture, and therefore its elements, in favor of a more abstract nonrepresentational formal system, leads to the progressive elimination of certain elements. One of the clearest examples of this is that of the liberation of the "plane" from the façade, whereby the wall becomes a skin, giving way to the elimination of the classical notion of the window.

With the modern movement and the development of abstract thought and the tendency toward abstraction, not only have styles been banished but also the need for figuration; thus on the one hand the image is related to the new theories of perception postulated by gestalt psychology, and on the other hand, meanings are achieved as they relate to abstract notions of geometry and physics.[7]

The language of architecture, in a classical sense, is destroyed. Fragments of languages develop with a more or less unified vocabulary, but certainly not as a consistent language. Technical developments advance a new aesthetic which dispenses with some of the major elements of classical language, such as openings. One of these developments, a major one, is the possibility of a structure independent from the walls. Domino is a prime example of this. The window, as it was known in a figurative sense, now has the possibility of disappearing and taking upon itself any imaginable configuration and composition with other windows. With this, the wall becomes an independent element which may be treated in any desired manner. The window will ultimately disappear altogether in order to

Machine Changing Men into Animals.

transform the building into either one big window or no window at all. Glass, already used as a technological device developed in the nineteenth century together with cast iron, and used mostly for functional or extravagant purposes (as in the Salons des Expositions Universelles or the Crystal Palace), now finds a theoretical support and acquires a new meaning.

It is clear, then, how various tendencies of the modern avant-garde coincided to propose an architecture of light and glass as the epitome of a new world. The elements of architectural language are no longer the elements of architecture, but rather the expression of volumetric organization as projections from inner images. The perception of representation and figuration in an historical sense is gone.

Two formal developments take place. One is the development of the glass box transformed from the irregular, *qum* expressionist, Mies skyscraper into the new classic form of the pure glass box. The other is a kind of superarticulated volumetric architecture, a play of volumes under light.

Mirror buildings seem to derive directly from the aesthetic form of the glass box at the start. With the illusory dematerialization of the wall, the architecture of mirrors is not only in complete opposition to classical architecture, but also creates an opposition within modern architecture.

Transparent clear glass suffers some transformations. First it is darkened, then it is mirrored; at this moment, a perfect opposition is established between glass and mirror. Glass architecture was part of an entire abstract formal system in which figuration and representation were brought to a minimum; when glass became mirror, this architecture was no longer consistent with the system from which it originated; it even questioned it. With mirror buildings we face a vocabulary derived from abstraction as a support for the most realistic of images, the mirrored ones.

It is probably not coincidental that the first mirror building, the Bell Laboratories by Eero Saarinen of 1962, was designed at one of the critical moments of modern architecture; a moment when the architecture of the glass box seemed it could go no further. The box remains the abstract entity, the pure form, and the pure function; no ornament, no figuration. The mirror, pure image applied to the box, takes charge of the figurative role. With this move, critical particularly in retrospect, a real crisis begins in that the separation between image and language in modern architecture becomes explicit. The mirror is pure image, but the image is not an architectural one. It is completely independent from the problem of figuration in architecture and from architectural codes.

An architecture of mirrors is also looking at other architectures and by force reflecting them, not as metaphoric representation but as literal reflection, and, as a most unusual condition, we have a mirror without its essential element: the subject. The specific context in which the building is inserted takes on the role occupied previously by the subject. This change from the relationship between subject and object to that between text and text exemplifies the break between classicism and modernity as a mode of symbolization.

The architecture of object by the use of mirrors paradoxically negates its own objecthood. This is clear particularly if one considers this architecture in context. The presence of the object is subdued by the fact that it attempts to absorb its context; it is object and context at the same time. Permeated by the qualities of its context, the building seems to replace, literally, its style and materials with an illusory image.

Mountain Bell Plaza, Phoenix, Arizona.
Alfred N. Beadle, architect, 1974.

While glass allowed for the visual social penetration of a building, the difference between public and private realms are now back in place. In a mirrored building, the only relationship established with the public realm is by reflection. The negation and elimination of the window precludes an interior/exterior relationship in the building. The building with windows relates more to the exterior than the building with a mirrored façade. Where glass established an almost symmetrical inside/outside relationship by means of the passage of light, mirrors put this relationship in frank opposition.

Although mirror architecture reflects the context, it is false contextualization. The object wrapped in mirror remains hermetic to the public world outside; thus the context is "locked" in the mirrored image and it becomes an "imaginary" context. The window has finally disappeared completely (as was intended by Scheerbart)[8] but the building has become hermetic, as though it is recuperating the lost stone wall.

The problem of contextualism is solved as the proof of reality that reconstructs the fragmented image of the city. Architecture has always been thought of as *corps morcelé* in relation to the city. The mirror buildings in an urban context seem to bring a certain recognition of unity to its fragmented body. The mirror building becomes a cutout of reality, and through its unifying reflection creates the illusion of coherence where in fact there is only a set of fragmentary relationships.

In a metonymic operation the mirror building becomes the city. As in Archimboldos's portraits, where the water is represented by a face made of fishes, shells, etc., the building is made of elements of the city—other buildings, ornaments, lights, cars, sidewalks, etc.—and becomes the city itself, or in instances where the sky and other natural elements are reflected, it becomes nature. In opposition to the classical mode of representation, representation becomes literal in this metonymic replacement.

The relationship between architectural language and image has not always been the same. At the time of Quatremère de Quincy, image and language went together in architecture. With the incorporation of the analogous image in architecture, there is a split between architectural language and image. The language of image opposes that of architecture.

The first mirror buildings were mostly boxes of different proportions, but always boxes with mirrored skins "dissolving" the building in pure image of messages without a code. Little by little another type of mirror building developed, one with more architectural articulation: a play of volumes, as though the box were not enough. Exemplary of this are the buildings of the 1970s by Pelli, Lumsden, Portman, and others. The conflicting relationship between language and image in architecture is now explicit. Mirror is situated between the realism of its images and the abstraction of the architectural configuration in its insertion in the history of modern architecture.

This new type of mirror building becomes skin architecture, even more than the box-like type. The Pacific Design Center in Los Angeles (1971) by Cesar Pelli is an example of this. The box and the skin seem to have developed together in a pure manner from the pure, minimal glass box. When the articulation of the volumes, still covered by a skin, starts to appear, the question of image or figuration and ab-

Bonaventure Hotel, Los Angeles, John Portman, architect.

Pacific Design Center, Los Angeles. Cesar Pelli, architect, 1971.

First International Building, Dallas, Texas (under construction). H. O. K., architects, 1974.

straction, in relation to architectural language, becomes an issue. In this sense the architecture of mirror is not very different from the decorated shed, or the architecture that makes use of styles or fragments of styles on its façade. They both bring into the scene of abstraction a figurative element of architectural representation, not at the level of architectural language, but of representation on the surface.

The architecture of the decorated skin claims a classic precedent representing architecture, and is thus pure code; it is code, however, with no language, thus no code. The mirror architecture comes from a modern source and is a realistic reflection/representation of the world, a message without a code. The image reflected on the mirror surface, just as the image in newspapers or photographs, is a message without a code, a continuous endless message. In these images of analogical reproductions of reality, a linguistic message is necessary to counteract or anchor their polysemous quality:[9] that is the role played by the architectural language in this later kind of mirror building. The architecture (or architectural language) becomes secondary to the image. It only serves to fix its meaning, just as verbal language would fix the uncertainty of the news image with its instantaneous, documentary quality.

In classical architecture, the mirror used in the interior not only relates to architectural language, but also to perspective and theatrical space, very much in tune with the explorations and concerns of the time, as they are represented in the works of the Bibiena; the subject is also at the center of this spatial exploration.

Now, the focus of architecture is image rather than language. In the mirrored buildings the articulation seems to be established with the arts of the image, such as photography and film. The image on the surface is filtered and unstable just like those projected on a screen. Here the subject has been displaced from the center, both in architecture and in film. "The film is like a mirror; it differs from the primordial mirror in one essential point. . . . There is one thing that is never reflected on it: the spectator's own body."[10] The surface is a kind of backdrop for a continuous documentary; a permanent set of realist images is projected onto the architecture, yet never touches it. The represented image is not consciously produced, but is a product of the particular conditions in which the building is set.

Indiana Bell Telephone Switching Center,
Columbus, Indiana. C. R. S. (Paul Kennon),
architect, 1979.

We are confronted now with the issue of meaning through image on a building or, more precisely, with the mode of signification in a building that is pure image. Mirror buildings produce a double effect of meaning by superimposing the architectural language and the mirror image on its surface, as may be seen in the Indiana Bell Building by Paul Kennon. Meaning is produced by the play between the architectural language (nonexistent in most instances) and the image reflected on the skin.

Architecture functions as meaning only at the level of architectural language, and it relates only through this to other languages or texts. Glass architecture is within this category; glass does not open to another signifying function for architecture, whereas mirror does. The inversion from glass to mirror is parallel to the change of emphasis from expressionism to surrealism. Perhaps this points to the reduction of meaning through the figurative illusion of transmitting more. The figurative level of the building is increased through the images, but at the same time the architectural specificity is reduced or negated.

L'Univers Démasqué. *René Magritte.*

Le Pays des Miracles. *René Magritte, c. 1960.*

The surrealist image and the documentary image meet in the architecture of mirrors with one common feature: the necessity of the word to support or complete the meaning of the image. The surrealist image needs the word to play with the codes of representation and the arbitrariness of language; the documentary image needs the word, the verbalized message, to anchor the meaning where there is no code. These two characteristics are synthesized in the effect produced by the mirror building when, in a documentary manner, it reflects the sky. A major inversion occurs: instead of the building cutting itself against the sky, building and sky are now one, as in Magritte's landscapes of reality.

In the Metropolitan Life Insurance Tower, an Italianate tower in New York of 1909, the glass in its double-hung windows has been replaced recently with mirror glass, creating the extraordinary effect of a hollow tower against the sky. Image and language have joined themselves here in a dialectical manner, symbolizing the transitional role of the architecture of mirror at this moment in the history of architecture.

Notes

1. Jacques Lacan, "Le stade du miroir comme formateur de la fonction du Je, telle qu'elle nous est révélée dans l'experience psychanalytique" *Ecrits* (Paris: Ed. du Seuil, 1966), pp. 92–100.

2. Quatremère de Quincy, *De l'imitation* (Paris, 1823).

3. Mario Gandelsonas, "Notes on Classical Architecture," theory course at the Institute for Architecture and Urban Studies, 1978.

4. Jurgis Baltrusaitis, "A Museé des Miroirs," *Macula 2* (1977).

5. Ibid.

6. Ibid.

7. Kurt Koffka, *Principles of Gestalt Psychology*; J. P. Sartre, *L'Imaginaire, psychologie phénoménologique de l'imagination* (Paris: Gallimard, 1960); E. H. Gombrich, *The Sense of Order: A Study in the Psychology of Decorative Arts* (Ithaca, N.Y.: Cornell University Press, 1979); Aloîss Riegl, *Problemi di Stile* (Milan: Feltrinelli Editore, 1963; original edition, St. Stilfragen, Berlin, 1893).

8. Paul Scheerbart, *Glasarchitektur* (Berlin: Verlag der Sturm, 1914).

9. Roland Barthes, "Le message photographique," *Communications 1* (Paris: Ed. du Seuil, 1963).

10. Roland Barthes, "La rhétorique de l'image," *Communications 4* (Paris: Ed. du Seuil, 1964).

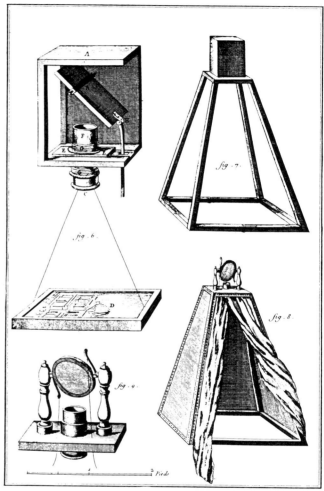

Des sein, Chambre Obscure.

Camera obscura: the image formed by the lens and reflected by the mirror on the ground glass is traced.

A room for representation or the representation of a room. A place for representation or the representation of a place; this is the camera obscura. A dark room where light penetrating through a small hole creates a whole world of illusion. The light is the shifter that permits transformation of the real into representation of the real, in one instant, at one point.[1] The fixation of that instant accounts for the history of photography. That point in time and space also accounts for a great deal of the history of Western architecture since the Renaissance and its concomitant problem of representation. That point that allows light to enter the camera obscura, creating an inverted image, is what ultimately links architecture and photography. Photography is a reflected image, but, as opposed to the simple inversion of the mirror image, it is further transformed by its technical manipulation, and especially by the framing that makes of the real a sign.

The camera obscura, literally a dark room that served as an aid for copying the *real* world, evolved into a movable chamber that could be placed outdoors, allowing the possibility of faithfully representing landscapes. The image reflected on the wall of this dark chamber served as a basis for painting not only landscapes but portraits as well. The camera obscura was already known in the Renaissance and was used as a tool to solve perspective problems. The first publication describing such a device is Giovanni Battista Della Porta's *Natural Magic* of 1558, in which the camera obscura is presented as an aid for drawing. In the seventeenth and eighteenth centuries the camera was standard equipment for artists. First a room of about ten square feet (big enough for a person to be inside), it was later made more sophisticated by reducing its size, adding lenses and a glass on the back, and incorporating mirrors to reverse the image.[2]

The question then arose of how to capture the fugitive image only apparently locked in this box, and together with this question emerged the powerful obsession to eliminate the intermediate system of representation, the drawing.

A number of experiments followed, including the development of the camera lucida, with the goal of fixing the image directly, by light itself, in the camera. In 1802 Thomas Wedgwood discovered how to print an image but not how to fix it. It was J. N. Niépce who in 1826 finally arrived at a way to fix the image produced in the camera. Several technical developments rapidly followed, of which the daguerreotype, invented by L. J. M. Daguerre in France in 1839, is the most famous.[3]

While the emphasis of this new medium was on technical discoveries and innovations, another problem was engendered concerning the position of this new mode of representation in relation to the visual arts in general and to painting in particular. Photography raised questions about the relation between *the real* and its representation. It is not only through painting but also through theater that photography relates to the art of representation. From the beginning the camera obscura was linked to the production of perspectival space in representational form. This was clear in many explorations of theatrical space made in the sixteenth and seventeenth centuries. "The camera obscura generated at one and the same time perspective painting, photography, and the Diorama, which are all three parts of the stage."[4] In its association with the stage photography touches upon architecture, which is in part the framing of a set of actions in space. But in contrast to theater, a photograph is always perceived as existing in the past; its very presence bespeaks absence. It is the document of a fugitive moment, a faraway place, or a lost being or object.[5] Thus for all of its technical reproducibility it is, if not itself unique, about the unique. In representing architecture, photography rewrites its history.

Architectural photography derives from the first decade of photography—the time of Hugo, Niépce, and Daguerre—before the "industrialization" of photography when, due to technical limitations, the camera could focus only on static structures, places, and buildings.[6] At that time, when technical preoccupations

Daguerre—the artist's studio. Daguerrotype, signed and dated 1837. Société Française de Photographie, Paris.

Camera lucida in use.

A Parisian Boulevard. *M. Daguerre.*
Daguerrotype, c. 1839.

prevailed over those of language, the photograph had the quality of a record, of a silent witness.

It was when photographic technique developed that the photographic surface as image took over and the codes of pictorial representation penetrated this new field, often only to blur it. From the popularized studio portraits with absurd background settings to the more sophisticated compositions emulating painting, the field of photography, from its birth to the beginning of the twentieth century, was denied its own specificity.

Photography was exhibited very much like painting in galleries both in Europe and America. But by the turn of the century a reaction to this pictorial approach ensued. In America the Photo-Secession group headed by Alfred Stieglitz and the journal *Camera Work*, which he founded in 1917, played fundamental roles and were seminal in developing the approach known as "straight photography."[7] This approach considered essential both the specificity of the medium and its autonomy from other forms of expression, namely painting.

Boulevard de Strasbourg, Corsets. *Eugène
Atget, 1912.*

Untitled. *Eugène Atget, 1912.*

For Stieglitz it was not necessarily the subject matter that made a photograph, but rather photography itself. This was stated explicitly in his "cloud photos," about which he said that clouds are there for everybody to see, whereas the image of the photo is not. The straight photography approach developed steadily and was strongly established by the 1920s (practiced by people like Paul Strand, Charles Sheeler, Edward Weston, and Ansel Adams).[8]

A figure essential to the history of photography who remained in obscurity under the prevailing pictorialist approach was Eugene Atget. Ignored by the pictorialists, he was given due credit just before his death in 1927.[9]

The work of Atget was that of a collector. He began photographing Paris in 1898, producing both a record and a very particular presentation of reality. The evocative quality of his work attracted the surrealists, who published it in the magazine *La Révolution Surréaliste* in 1925.[10] His technique was one common in the nineteenth century; he wandered through the city streets with his tripod and large camera, producing hundreds of photographs of different subjects. He saw what no other eye would see in the everyday life of the city—he was an "imagier," a kind of urban archeologist. The camera obscura became a Pandora's box when, reduced and made portable, it produced an image that could be fixed. But in the hands of Atget it became a magician's hat from which extraordinary objects appeared.

The element of surprise in the displacement of meaning, which is at the heart of magic, was used by the surrealists as a symbolic device and explains why they found in Atget a heroic figure. He came closest to "the real" and was thus a constant source of ready-mades. He had shown without much rhetoric that the camera, in confronting reality, was a tool that made the magical appear in the seeming banality of everyday life and places. His work thus emphasized *presentation* and *perception* rather than *representation* as modes of relating to the real—an opposition significant not only for photography itself and the avant-garde visual arts of the 1920s but also for architecture. The particular way in which the city with its places and buildings is presented in the work of Atget—in its nostalgic emptiness, in its uninhabited humanity, in its monumental stillness and suspension in time and space—seems to provide an absolute referent for architectural photography.

Untitled. *Eugène Atget, 1912.*

Untitled. *Eugène Atget, 1912.*

Untitled. *Eugène Atget, 1912.*

Beau comme la rencontre fortuite, sur une table de dissection, d'une machine à coudre et d'un parapluie. *Man Ray, 1933.*

A great amount of photographic work was produced in the 1920s in the context of the artistic avant-garde. Some of this work emphasized formal aspects, some of the symbolic potential of the photographic image. Moholy-Nagy and Man Ray were paradigmatic of the two tendencies. The opposition between the two approaches is the key to the exploration of an issue that once again closely links the questions surrounding both photography and architecture, for it brings to center stage the problem of abstraction versus representation, or even more, the question of the real versus the representation of the real (one could even say the question of image and language).[11] The tendency represented by Moholy-Nagy was directed toward the expression of a rational formal language underlying the mere appearance of things. Thanks to the new vision made possible by the lens, photography could now parallel painting and other arts. The problem of the surrealists on the other hand was one of figuration, not as representation but as unmediated capturing of the real: the ready-made. André Breton and Man Ray saw in photography the most essential mode of expression other than the word.[12]

This approach points to the possibility of an unmediated relationship between the real and its photographic image—to speech rather than language. The narrative

Untitled. *Man Ray, 1928.*

that derives from the evocative or connotative power of surrealist photographic images is open, and in a certain symbolic explicitness it becomes an indicator of the mechanisms of codification and recodification at play in the dangerous game of representation. By getting as close as possible to the "real object," an effect of distance is produced.

Architectural photography—or better, architecture through photography—shares some ground with surrealist photography, if not with surrealism, in that particular quality of the ready-made and of the grouping of photographs of buildings and places to create a repertory of found objects. In the photography of architecture is the potential for that moment of silence when everything disappears and we enter another world—more like entering a text than a finished work—where a sentimental relationship is established with the image, "framed like a caged bird," and where places become "inhabitable rather than visible."[13]

The frame and framing play major roles in photography.[14] Atget creates a tremor around the frame; cutting and framing is an act of fragmentation of the real, of incorporating the real in a classifying discourse. Architectural photography per se is a structure *en abyme*, the representation of a representation, for it frames reality itself. The frame was essential to the surrealists' will for disclosure of the symbolic performance of the image and its perception: framing was the indication of the arbitrariness of meaning and allowed for a metaphoric recording of reality as fragment. Framing in the work of Moholy-Nagy and his peers instead became a syntactical compositional device: the real was the referent of a representation that was strongly influenced by codes still related to painting.

Architectural photography as an image of architecture allows us to address this question, for we are faced with images while simultaneously confronted with specific formal mechanisms at play in the architectural discourse. The issue of image and language superimposes the specificity of photography on the specificity of architecture.

Many avenues of thought can be followed in facing the issue of architecture and photography. The one that seems to be pertinent today is that touching upon the relationship between image and language, or between perception and representa-

Rue Sade, Antibes. *Man Ray, 1936.*

Marseille, 1929. *Moholy-Nagy.*

1929. *Moholy-Nagy.*

Fagus Factory, Alfeld, Germany. Walter Gropius, architect. Photograph by Roberto Schezen, 1982.

tion. Architecture and photography traditionally have been closely linked. After their respective complex historical developments, they come together again now that all representation of the real is possible, in the face of the need for critical discourse on the conditions of representation today.

Some years ago I was involved in the most surreal of photographic sessions, the photographing of a blind man. He was facing a camera that he could not see, and for me, seeing through him as for him at that moment, the visual world went out to focus and only the word prevailed. The man was Jorge Luis Borges, whose world was that of the word, and thus the visual world of objects was the world of the text that incessantly came out of him. Photographing Borges is like photographing architecture, a blind witness that is itself a text. It is with the notion of text that we can go beyond the simplistic dichotomy between abstraction and figuration that permeates the discourse on representation in architecture today.

Notes

1. For the notion of shifter as a recording device, see "Design versus Non-Design," this volume.

2. Beaumont Newhall, *The History of Photography: 1839 to the Present* (New York: Museum of Modern Art, 1964); Raymond Lecuyer, *Histoire de la photographie* (Paris: Bascher & Co., 1945).

3. Newhall, *The History of Photography: 1839 to the Present.*

4. Roland Barthes, *Camera Lucida* (New York: Hill and Wang, 1981).

5. Ibid.

6. Walter Benjamin, "Une petite histoire de la photographie," *Essais 1: 1922–34* (Paris: De Noel-Gonthier, 1955).

7. Newhall, *History of Photography.*

8. Ibid.

9. Arthur D. Trottenberg, ed., *A Vision of Paris: The Photographs of Eugene Atget, The Words of Marcel Proust* (New York: Macmillan, 1963).

10. Berenice Abbott, who was then working with Man Ray in Paris, was instrumental in making his work known.

11. Andreas Haus, *Photographs and Photograms: Moholy-Nagy* (New York: Pantheon, 1980); Philippe Sers, ed., *Man Ray: Photographe* (Paris, 1981).

12. Rosalind Krauss, "Photography in the Service of Surrealism," in Rosalind Krauss and Jane Livingston, eds., *L'Amour Fou: Photography and Surrealism* (New York: Abbeville Press, 1985).

13. Barthes, *Camera Lucida.*

14. Krauss, "Photography in the Service of Surrealism."

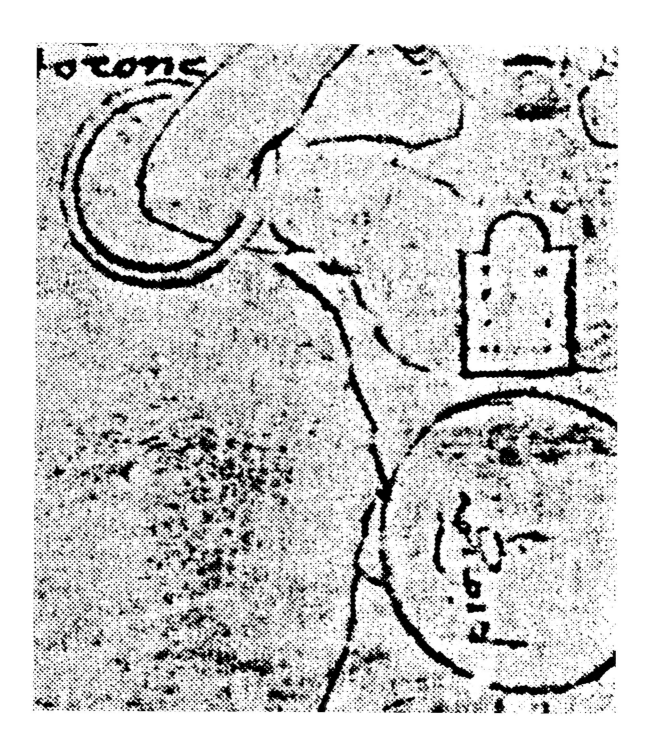

Somewhere every culture has an imaginary zone for what it excludes, and it is this zone that we must try to remember today.[1]

For something to be excluded, two parts are necessary: something inside, some defined entity, and something outside. In our world of architectural ideology there is such an inside: the body of texts and rules developed in the Renaissance that, as a reading of the classics, established the foundations for Western architecture, which I call the "system of architecture." This inside has been transformed throughout history, at some times more profoundly than at others, and even through the apparent breaks of the first decades of this century it has remained at the very base of Western architectural thought.

Logocentrism and anthropomorphism, in particular male anthropomorphism, are underlying the system of architecture since Vitruvius, then read and rewritten in the Renaissance and through the modern movement.[2] This system is not only defined by what it includes, but also by what it excludes; inclusion and exclusion are parts of the same construct. That which is excluded, left out, is not really excluded but rather repressed; repression neither excludes nor repels an exterior force, for it contains within itself an interior of representation, a space of repression.[3] That repressed, that interior representation in the system of architecture that determines an outside (of repression) is woman and woman's body. The ideological construct of the architectural system determined by an idealistic logic and a concomitant system of repressions becomes apparent in the role sex plays within it. The logic in the system of architecture represses sex in two different ways: sex is thought of in both positive and negative terms; where woman is assigned the negative term (phallocentrism), and sex is neutralized or erased through the medium of the artist who, sexless, engenders by himself and gives birth to a work, the product of creation.[4]

Society established a certain kind of symbolic order where not everyone can equally fit. There are those who do fit and those who have to find their place between symbolic orders, in the interstices; they represent a certain symbolic instability. These are the people often called odd, abnormal, or perverse or who have been labeled neurotics, ecstatics, outsiders, witches, or hysterics.[5] In strange ways, woman has been placed in this category when she has tried to establish her presence rather than limit herself to finding a way of "fitting" within the established symbolic order.

Woman has been allowed to surface from the space of her repression as a witch or a hysteric and thus has been burned or locked up, ultimately representing the abnormal.[6] Women, who are the bearers of the greatest norm, that of reproduction, paradoxically also embody the anomaly.[7] It is through her body and through the symbolic order that woman has been repressed in architecture, and in dealing with body and architecture the obvious question—what body?—is the key to the unveiling of many mysterious ideological fabrications. Asking "what body?" is synonymous to asking "which gender?" for a genderless body is an impossible body.

In many of the important texts of the Renaissance, the founding texts of Western architectural ideology, the subject of the body in architecture is not only essential but moreover is indissolubly linked to the question of gender and sex, a question that has generated the most extraordinary architectural metaphors in the elaboration of architectural ideology. The reading of those texts is an essential operation in the understanding of a complex ideological apparatus that has systematically excluded woman, an exclusion made possible by an elaborate mechanism of symbolic appropriation of the female body.

Two scenes will be presented here, two scenes of architecture:

Scene I: The Book of the Renaissance

Scene II: The Text of the City

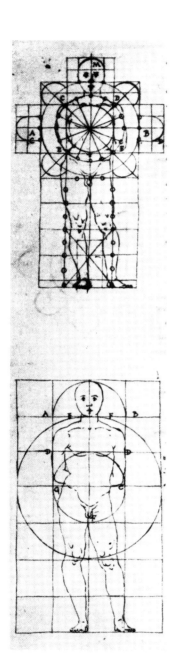

Anthropomorphic proportioning in the design of a temple with a longitudinal plan, dividing the height of the human body in seven or nine parts. Francesco di Giorgio Martini.

Scene I: The Book of the Renaissance

The Scene of the Repressed: Architecture from Within

Architecture in the Renaissance establishes a system of rules that is the basis of Western architecture. The texts of the Renaissance, which in turn read the classic texts from Vitruvius, develop a logocentric and anthropocentric discourse establishing the male body at the center of the unconscious or architectural rules and configurations. The body is inscribed in the system of architecture as a male body replacing the female body. The Renaissance operations of symbolization of the body are paradigmatic of the operations of repression and exclusion of woman by means of the replacement of her body. Woman not only has been displaced/replaced at a general social level throughout the history of architecture, but more specifically, at the level of body and architecture.

Architecture as a Representation of the Body

The texts of the Renaissance offer a certain clue to the mode in which the appropriation by man of woman's place and body in architecture has taken place in a complex process of symbolization that works at the level of architectural ideology, therefore at an almost unconscious level. Several texts are exemplary of this procedure in varying degrees, particularly Alberti's *Ten Books on Architecture*, Filarete's *Treatise on Architecture*, and Francesco Di Giorgio Martini's *Architettura Civile e Militare* and *Architettura Ingegneria e Arte Militare*, and of course we cannot forget Vitruvius, whose *Ten Books of Architecture* are at the base of every Renaissance text.

In the several steps in the operation of symbolic transference from the body to architecture, the first is the relationship established between man and nature through the notions of natural harmony and perfection.[8] Man is presented as having the attribute of perfect natural proportions. Thus the analogical relationship between architecture and the human body appears to ensure that the natural laws of beauty and nature are transferred into architecture. The body thus becomes a mediator, a form of "shifter."[9]

It is in Vitruvius that we first find the important notions that are to be reelaborated in various ways in other later texts. His text clearly posits the issue of the human body as a model for architecture, particularly in his chapter "On Symmetry in

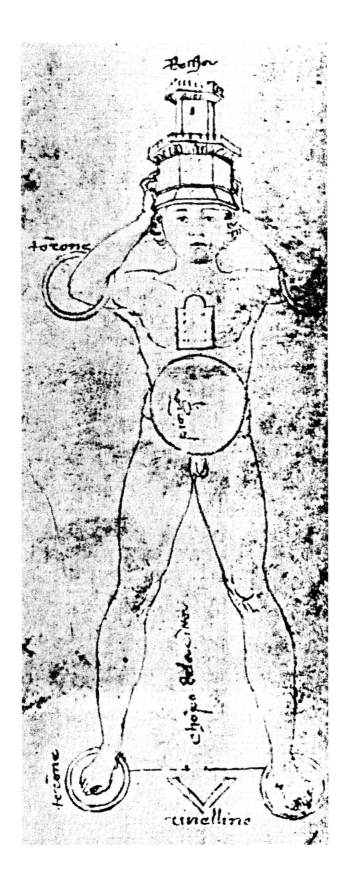

Disegno della Similitudine fra Uomo e Città.
Francesco di Giorgio Martini, 1482.

Temples and the Human Body," where symmetry is related to proportion—symmetry being an essential feature in the design of temples and proportion being the correspondence among measures of an entire work.

Without symmetry and proportion, that is, if there is no precise relation between the members as in "a well-shaped man," there can be no principles of design. Furthermore, the measurements for buildings are all to be derived from the members of the body. The design of a temple depends on symmetry, the principles of which must be carefully observed by the architect. They are due to proportion, in Greek "avanoyia." Proportion is a correspondence among measures of the members of an entire work, and of the whole to a certain part selected as standard. From this results the principles of symmetry. Without symmetry and proportion there can be no principles in the design of any temple; that is, if there is no precise relation between its members, as in the case of those of a well-shaped man. Further, it was from the members of the body that they derived the fundamental ideas of the measures which are obviously necessary in all works, as the finger, palm, foot and cubit.[10]

The relationship between architecture and the human body becomes particularly important at the moment in which the issue of the center, a preoccupation that filters throughout the history of art and architecture in its many symbolic roles, acquires a very specific meaning.

Then again, in the human body the central point is naturally the navel. For if a man be placed flat on his back, with his hands and feet extended, and a pair of compasses centered at his navel, the fingers and toes of his two hands and feet will touch the circumference of a circle described therefrom. And just as the human body yields a circular outline, so too a square figure may be found from it. For if we measure the distance from the soles of the feet to the top of the head, and then apply measure to the outstretched arms, the breadth will be found to be the same as the height, as in the case of plane surfaces which are perfectly square.[11]

The center is represented by the navel, which becomes a metonymic object or a "shifter" in relation to gender. It is a true shifter in that it transforms the body into geometry, nature into architecture, the "I" of the subject into the "I" of the discourse. The relationship between these two "I's" is what allows the constant shift-

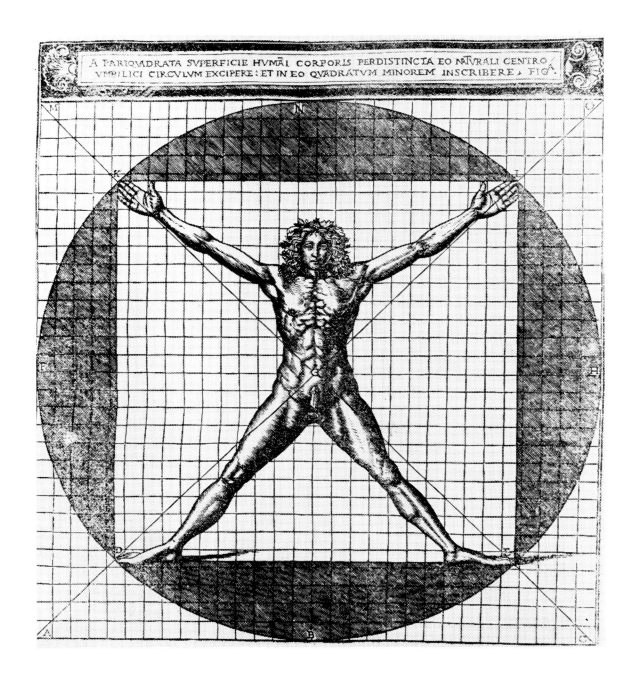

Uomo ad Circulum. *Cesariano, 1611.*

ing of genders. This type of formal relationship between the body of man and architecture, developed by Vitruvius, will be ever-present in the Renaissance texts.

An analogical relationship between the body (of man) and architecture can also be found in Alberti's *Ten Books on Architecture*:

The whole Force of the invention and all our skill and Knowledge in the Art of Building, it is required in the Compartition: Because the distinct Parts of the entire Building, and, to use such a Word, the Entireness of each of those parts and the Union and Agreement of all the lines and Angles in the Work, duly ordered for Convenience, Pleasure and Beauty are disposed and measured out by the Compartition alone: For if a City, according to the Opinion of Philosophers, be no more than a great House and, on the other hand, a House be a little City; why may it not be said that the Members of that House are so many little Houses . . . and as the Members of the Body are correspondent to each other, so it is fit that one part should answer to another in a Building; whence we say, that great Edifices require great Members.[12]

Alberti is never as direct in his analogies as Vitruvius or as other architects of the Renaissance. His text offers a far more elaborate system of metaphorical transformation by which he develops specific notions that allow for the development of an abstract system in a discourse that incorporates the "laws of nature."

If what we have here laid down appears to be true, we may conclude Beauty to be such a Consent and Agreement of the Parts of the Whole in which it is found, as to Number, Finishing and Collocation, as Congruity, that is to say, the principal law of Nature requires. This is what Architecture chiefly aims at, and by this she obtains her Beauty, Dignity and Value. The Ancients knowing from the Nature of Things, that the Matter was in fact as I have stated it, and being convinced, that if they neglected this main Point they should never produce any Thing great or commendable, did in their Works propose to themselves chiefly the Imitation of Nature, as the greatest Artist at all Manner of Compositions. . . . Reflecting therefore upon the Practice of Nature as well with Relation to an entire Body, as to its several Parts, they found from the very first Principles of Things, that Bodies were not always composed of equal parts or Members; whence it happens, that of the Bodies produced by Nature, some are smaller, some are larger, and some middling.[13]

The process of symbolization takes place by relating the body as a system of proportion to other systems of proportion. The body, transformed into an abstract system of formalization, is thus incorporated into the architectural system as form, through the orders, hierarchies, and the general system of formal organization allowing for this anthropocentric discourse to function at the level of the unconscious.

Transsexual Operations in Architecture

Vitruvius and Alberti point the way to the incorporation of the body as an analogue, model, or referent, elaborating a system for its transformation into a system of architectural syntactic rules, elements, and meanings. In the work of Filarete and Francesco Di Giorgio Martini, the original ambiguity of the gender of the body in question is eliminated by making explicit the fact that human figure is synonymous with male figure. A different ambiguity will appear instead, the ambiguity of the gender or sex itself. In a rather complex set of metaphorical operations throughout these texts, the gender of the body and its sexual functions are exchanged in a move of cultural transsexuality whereby man's ever-present procreative fantasy is enacted.

Filarete starts by making sure that we understand not only that architecture is directly linked to the human figure but that when he refers to "human" figure or body, it is the male figure:

As I have said, the building is constructed as a simile for the human figure. You see that I have shown you by means of a simile that a building is derived from man, that is, from his form, members, and measure. . . . Now as I have told you above, I will show you how the building is given form and substance by analogy with the members and form of man. You know that all buildings need members and passages, that is, entrances and exits. They should all be formed and arranged according to their origins. The exterior and interior appearance of the building is arranged effectively in such a way that the members and passages are suitably located, just as the exterior and interior parts and members are correct for the body of man.[14]

The conditions are here for the development of a double analogy and for possible exchanges and combinations in the body considered as interior and/or exterior. In

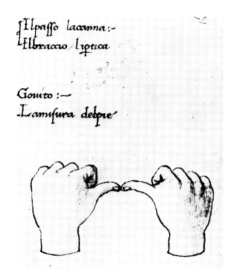

Unità di Misura. *Filarete, c. 1460.*

the most common and apparent analogical relationship between the body of man and architecture, we are faced with the exterior. In bringing about the interior, another set of metaphors will be possible, particularly those that allow for the permutation of the genders. To be able to elaborate on the questions of the interior of man, Filarete does not stop at the formal analogy; his symbolic operations lead him to develop his most extraordinary metaphor, that of the building as living man:

(When they are) measured, partitioned and placed as best you can, think about my statements and understand them clearly. I will (then) show you (that) the building is truly a living man. You will see it must eat in order to live, exactly as it is with man. It sickens or dies or sometimes is cured of its sickness by a good doctor[15]. . . . In the first book you have seen, as I have demonstrated to you, the origins of the building and its origins in my opinion, how it is proportioned to the human body of man, how it needs to be nourished and governed and through lack it sickens and dies like man.[16]

In this manner he slowly and steadily builds up a symbolic argument that unfolds from the building created as a formal analogue of the male body, from which even the orders are derived, to the building as a living body. If the building is a living man, the next necessary step in the argument is its conception and birth. It is at this critical point that another body will be incorporated: that of the architect himself.

You perhaps could say, you have told me that the building is similar to man. Therefore, if this is so it needs to be conceived and then born. As (it is) with man himself, so (it is) with the Building. First it is conceived, using a simile such as you can understand, and then it is born. The mother delivers her child at the term of nine months or sometimes seven; by care and in good order she makes him grow.[17]

If the building is a living man, someone has to give birth to it. The figure of the architect becomes feminized in the act of procreation:

The building is conceived in this manner. Since no one can conceive himself without a woman, by another simile, the building cannot be conceived by one man alone. As it cannot be done without woman, so he who wishes to build needs an architect. He conceives it with him and then the architect carries it. When the ar-

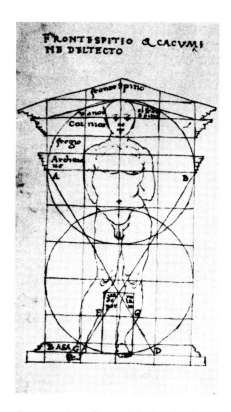

Proportioning scheme of the facade of a temple with a longitudinal plan. Francesco di Giorgio Martini.

chitect has given birth he becomes the mother of the building. Before the architect gives birth, he should dream about his conception, think about it, and turn it over in his mind in many ways for seven to nine months, just as a woman carries her child in her body for seven or nine months. He should also make various drawings of this conception that he has made with the patron, according to his own desires. As the woman can do nothing without the man, so the architect is the mother to carry this conception. When he has pondered and considered and thought (about it) in many ways, he ought to choose, (according to his own desires), what seems most suitable and most beautiful to him according to the terms of the patron. When this birth is accomplished, that is when he has made, in wood, a small relied design of its final form, measured and proportioned to the finished building, then he shows it to the father.[18]

Filarete takes this transsexual operation to its extreme by transforming the architect into a woman (or better, mother). He proceeds to state that, just like a mother, the architect also has to be a nurse, and "with love and diligence" he will help the building grow to its completion. And just as a mother who loves her sons and with the help of the father tries to make them good and beautiful, the architect should make his buildings good and beautiful.

As I have compared the architect to the mother, he also needs to be nurse. He is both mother and nurse. As the mother is full of love for her son, so he will rear it with love and diligence, cause it to grow, and bring it to completion if it is possible; if it is not, he will leave it ordered.[19]

Filarete will take this argument all the way in order to cover the various aspects involved in the building:

A good mother loves her son and with the aid of the father strives to make him good and beautiful, and with a good master to make him valiant and praiseworthy. So the good architect should strive to make his buildings good and beautiful.[20]

Woman is excluded (repressed) in a first move by making architecture an image of man as an analogue to man's body and, as we have seen, to the point of making it a living organism. Woman is then replaced—her place usurped by man who as the architect has the female attributes necessary for the conception and reproduction—in an extraordinary operation that I call here architectural transsexuality, for which the repression of woman is essential.

Filarete's texts are greatly complemented by those of Francesco Di Giorgio Martini. In his *Trattati: Architettura Civile e Militare* and *Architettura Ingegneria e Arte Militare*, Di Giorgio uses similar analogies between the human body and architecture, but in this case the analogy is proposed at the scale of the city.

One should shape the city, fortress, and castle in the form of a human body, that the head and the attached members have a proportioned correspondence and that the head be the rocca, the arms its recessed walls, which, circling around, link the rest of the whole body, the vast city. . . . And thus it should be considered that just as the body has all its members and parts in perfect measurements and proportions, in the composition of temples, cities, fortresses, and castles the same principles should be observed.[21]

This argument is developed further by Di Giorgio in a more specific way, so that this ideology can be better translated into specific formal systems:

Cities have the reasons, measurements, and form of the human body; I am going to describe precisely their perimeters and partitions. First, the human body stretched on the ground should be considered. Placing a string at the navel, the other end will create a circular form. This design will be squared and angles placed in similar fashion. . . . Thus it should be considered just as the body has all the parts and members in perfect measurement and circumference, the center in the cities and other buildings should be observed. . . . The palms and the feet would constitute other temples and squares. And as the eyes, ears, nose and mouth, the veins, intestines, and other internal parts and members are organized inside and outside the body according to its needs, in the same way this should be observed in cities, as we shall show in some focus.[22]

The reading and reuse of Vitruvius takes a new dimension in Francesco Di Giorgio, for it is not only part of an analogical discourse between body (male) and the city, it is at the same time central in a representational discourse where the roles and places of male and female body in relation to architecture are swiftly exchanged. It is in shifting from the external appearance to the internal functions and order of the body that we will be faced once more with a transsexual operation:

And so as it has been said that all the internal parts (of the human body) are orga-

Il Monte Athos. *Francesco di Giorgio Martini.*

nized and divided for its government and subsistence, in the same way that inside and outside parts of the body are necessary; it is that each member of the city should be distributed to serve its subsistence, harmony, and government.[23]

I therefore say that first of all the main square (piazza) should be placed in the middle and the center of that city or as close as possible, just as the navel is to man's body; convenience should go second to this. The reason for this similitude could be the following; just as it is through his navel that human nature gets nutrition and perfection in its beginnings, in the same way by this common place the other particular places are served.[24]

This can only be an analogy after some operations of substitution are performed. In relation to the umbilical cord (the tie to the mother, the woman), Di Giorgio says, "like the navel is to a man's body." However, the relationship of the man's body to the umbilical cord is one of dependence. It is not he who is providing nourishment: rather, it is he who is being nourished by the mother at the beginning of life. Thus for the analogy to work for the city, the female body should be taken as the symbolic reference; instead the male body occupies its place. The female body is replaced by the male body, and man's navel is transformed into the city's "womb." Man's body is functionally transformed, feminized, in the production of this architectural analogy.

Although the sexual organs are never mentioned, they have an analogical presence in some of Di Giorgio's designs for cities, where the male sexual organ occupies the place and parts previously analogically assigned to the various parts of the body. That which has been taken must be negated; it is the denial that goes with repression.

I propose that there are three instances in this play of substitutions:
· The male body is projected, represented, and inscribed in the design of buildings and cities and in the texts that establish their ideology. The female body is suppressed or excluded.
· The architect himself is presented as a woman in relation to the reproductive creative functions, operating as a "literal" sexual replacement.
· The male body becomes female body in its functions of giving nourishment—that is, life—to the city; man's navel becomes woman's womb.

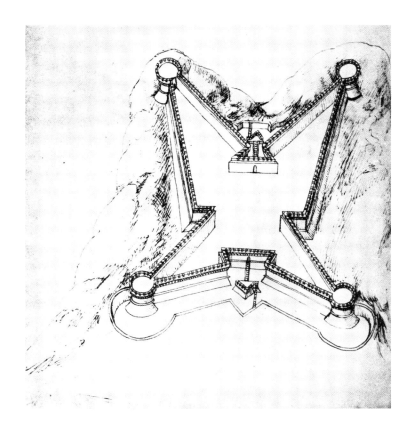

Fortress on two contiguous hills. Francesco di Giorgio Martini.

Configuration of the perimeter of a fortress between mountains and plain. Francesco di Giorgio Martini.

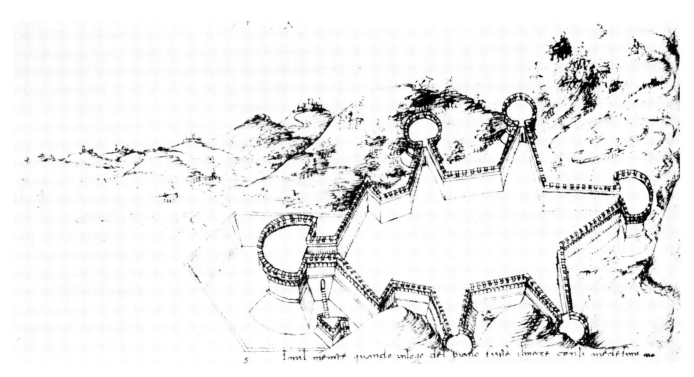

Plan of two circular rocche *together.*
Francesco di Giorgio Martini.

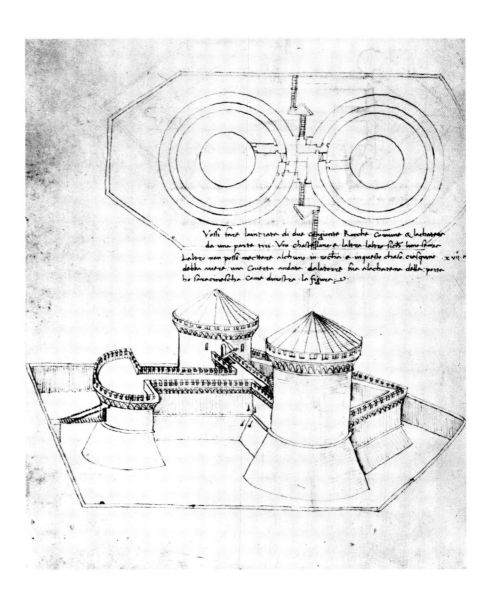

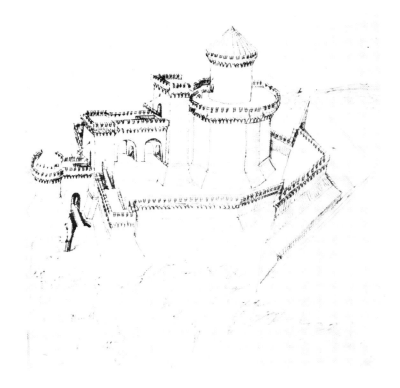

Pentagonal fortress. Francesco di Giorgio Martini.

Rocca with triangular master tower. Francesco di Giorgio Martini.

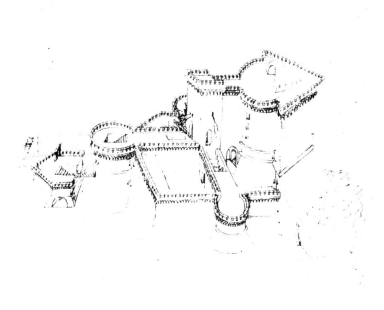

It is remarkable that the replacement of the female body by the male body always occurs in relation to the maternal function, reproduction. It has been said that we live in a civilization in which the consecrated-religious or secular representation of femininity is subsumed by the maternal.[25] In this perspective, the whole operation appears to be a veiled representation of the myth of Mary.

In Filarete, the architect, a man, gives birth like a woman. In Di Giorgio, the center of the city, based on the configuration of man's body, gives subsistence through the umbilical cord from the womb, like a woman's body, to the rest of the city. In one case men's fantasies of conception and reproduction are placed in the figure of the architect, in the other they are set in the principles organizing the formal configuration of the city. Woman is thus suppressed, repressed, and replaced.

Suppressed, in the analogical relation between body and architecture. It is man's body—that is, according to the classic texts, the natural and perfectly proportioned body—from which architectural principles and measurements derive.

Repressed, in the model of the city. Woman's unique quality, that of motherhood, is projected onto the male body. Thus woman is not only suppressed, but indeed her whole sexual body is repressed.

Replaced, by the figure of the architect. The male, through what I have called before a transsexual operation, has usurped the female's reproductive qualities in the desire to fulfill the myth of creation.

It is motherhood that is taken more than woman, but motherhood has always been confused with womanhood as one and the same: the representation of femininity is subsumed by the maternal.[26]

In the art of the Renaissance, Mary, Queen of the Heavens and Mother of the Church, is an ever-present figure. Fantasies of conception by men could also be found in the texts by other men, including St. Augustine. It is within the context of Christianism that the treatises of Alberti, Di Giorgio Martini, and Filarete were developed. The power of this religious ideology was evidenced in the mode of representation of religion and its concomitant myths. A most powerful one was that of the Virgin Mary. The nature of the mother/son relationship between Mary and Christ and the belief in immaculate conception leads toward the possibility of pregnancy without sex: woman, rather than being penetrated by a male, conceives with a nonperson, the spirit.[27] This conception without sex (sin) is the negation of sex as an essential part in the reproductive process, and ultimately, in the birth of Christ.

This religious ideology was all-encompassing. In a move of perfect ideological representation in a particular subregion of ideology, that of architecture, the architect can give birth to buildings or cities by usurping the female body, and just like Mary he can conceive without sex, only through spirit. Man is thus placed at the center of creation.

The treatises of architecture mentioned develop a system of rules elaborating an ideology that allows for the transformations in philosophy, Christianism, and the structure of power of the church to filter through the subregion of architecture.[28]

Woman (mother/Mary) is necessary as an imposing image within the system; woman outside that system, if not suppressed, had to be burned. Mary on one hand, heretics and witches on the other (those who pointed out the system of repressions and the possibility of a certain demystification). Men's mechanism of the assumption of the maternal role, through Christianism, may also be a mechanism of masculine sublimation.[29]

Scene II: The Text of the City

The Return of the Repressed: Architecture from Without

The system of architecture from within is characterized by an idealistic logic that can assume neither contradiction nor negation and therefore is based upon the suppression of either one or two opposite terms. This is best represented by the consistent repression of woman. Woman is excluded; she does not fit in the symbolic order. She is offside, in the cracks of symbolic systems; she has been called a witch, a hysteric, an outsider.[30]

It is in that outside that she stands. It is from that outside that she can project better than anyone the critical look. Woman can place herself from without the system of architecture by accepting heterogeneity and thus the positive inclusion of the negated, woman, the formerly repressed. In the ideological realm of architecture this implies a negation of the "system of architecture" through a critical work, and the inclusion of the denied, the excluded, the hidden, the repressed.

This discourse from without incorporates heterogeneous matter, includes negation, and is psychoanalytical and historical. Woman, representing both heterogeneity of matter through her body and historical negation of her gender, is in the perfect position to develop such a discourse. Woman, a discourse of heterogeneity, "represents the negative in the homogeneity of the community."[31]

Taking a place from without the system is not only to include what has been negated, or excluded, or to surface the repressed; a more complex process takes place. The classic architectural project of the city (as a body) is a reflection in the mirror of a totally formed, closed, and unitary system. We are dealing now with the modern city instead, with a representation of a fragmented body.[32] The architect cannot recognize himself or his system of rules in the mirror of the city as did Di Giorgio or Filarete. The body as a metaphor of the fragmented architectural body, which cannot be recomposed within the system of architectural rules, will be that referential outside.

It is the explosion, the fragmented unconscious, where the "architectural body" does not reflect the body of the subject, as it did in the Renaissance, but reflects instead the perception of the fragmented body as the built text, a set of fragments of languages and texts, the city. The body cannot be reconstructed, the subject—architect/man—does not recognize himself in architecture as an entity in front of the mirror. The system has been broken; architecture cannot be recognized again as a whole.

We will take that built social unconscious of architecture, the city, a text, for it is not the result of the creation of a subject/product of a logocentric, anthropomorphic system. There is no subject there. Here are only fragments of text and languages to be read, and in this reading they traverse the subject, in the position of reader-writer.

The Street: Streetwalkers
The city presents itself as a fragmentary text escaping the order of things and of language, a text to be "exploded," taken in pieces, in fragments, to be further decomposed in so many possible texts, open in a metonymy of desire.

To design is not to reclose but to affect the openings and be affected by them, to play an intersection between the two subjects, that of the reader and that of the writer, by an operation of shifting through the "I." The subject gets caught in the text and becomes part of the text.

This subject, woman, writes as she reads where the repression has failed, where the system is fragmented, and where she does not want to be reconstructed by finding in it the reflection of an enclosed homogeneous unitary system. She reads there and activates the absence of the repression/replacement of her body.

The street is the scene of her writing, with her body following the role that she is given in the evaluation of her body as merchandise. The street is the scene of architectural writing. The private realm is the scene of the institutions, where woman and her body have an assigned place: the house.

Wife in the kitchen. Whore in the street.

Rather than worshiping the monuments, we take the streets, we "play house," taking a critical view of the family as a hierarchical system and of the rules of architecture that go with it.

The city is the social scene where woman can publicly express her struggle. She was/is not accepted in the institutions of power, she is dispossessed (of her body) and is with the dispossessed. The public place is a no-man's-land ready to be appropriated. The scene of the city, of the street, of the public place, is that of the dispossessed; it is there where she is "at home."

(A place outside the accepted institutions is taken and assumed through various texts and readings of an open and heterogeneous quality.)

Reading from Without
I think of these projects. I have a vision, a realist image of unreal events. It flows without knowing like a mystic pad; the city like an unconscious of architecture unveils itself, three modes of time in three analogues of experience: permanence, succession, simultaneity.

A register of urban inscriptions, these three together—now I am reading, now I am writing—the boundaries are not clear. I can read the words, the unsaid, the hid-

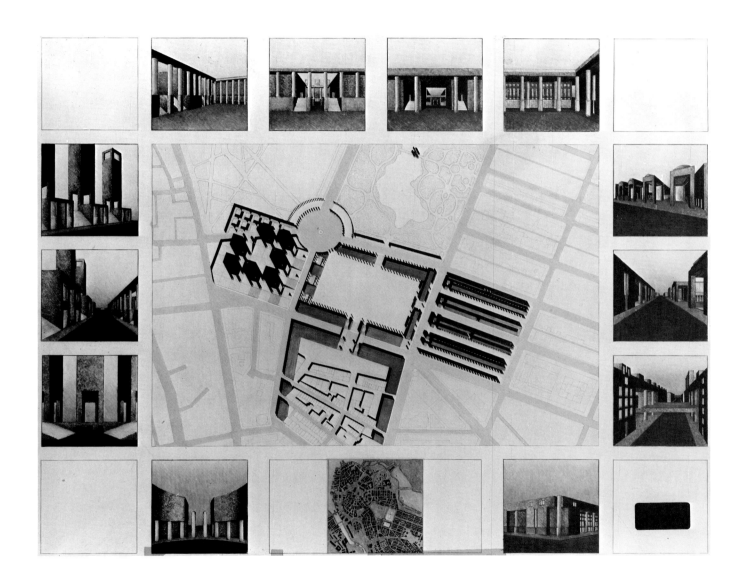

Park Square, Boston. Project by Diana
Agrest.

den, there where no man wants to read, where there are no monuments to speak of an established and unitary system of architecture.

Like an optical illusion the grid becomes an object, then the fabric, then the object again. The apparent contradiction and undialectical opposition between object and fabric at the base of this process develops a text from the inclusions and juxtaposition of these opposite terms.

All of a sudden an erasure, the erasure necessary to remark, reinstates the obvious not seen, the tabula rasa that could become fabric, the object that would rather be a public place.

The "refoules" (repressed) of architecture, the public, the negation, all become the material of my fictional configuration. The (project) marks I make are organized through a contradiction—a negation through an affirmation. Negate the city to affirm the city. It is the affirmation of the erasure of the city in order to reinstate its trace. The critical reading is taking from the subject: I am spoken through the city, through architecture, and the city is read through me.

Notes

This text originated in the fall of 1971 as a proposal for an article, "Architecture from Without: Matter, Logic, and Sex," to be published in an architectural journal. Although my interest was very strong at that time, I did not have the opportunity to develop it until 1986–87.

Although the original abstract was only four pages long, it contained all of the elements (arguments) necessary to develop this article. During the process of this development I realized that the first part, "Architecture from Within," could be expanded, whereas the second part, "Architecture from Without," could not be expanded in the same manner. The reason for this is that the latter posits a premise for critical work and a way of approaching it. I believe that this critical approach to architecture is present in my work produced throughout the years in practice, theory, criticism, and teaching.

I want to thank Judy O'Buck Gordon for her incentive and her persistent interest in the development of this essay.

1. Catherine Clément, "La Coupable," in *La Jeune Née* (Paris, Union Général d'Editions, 1975), p. 6.

2. Even the Modulor by Le Corbusier is entirely based on a male body.

3. Jacques Derrida, "Freud et la Scène de l'Ecriture," in *L'Ecriture et la Différence* (Paris: Editions du Seuil, 1967).

4. Julia Kristeva, "Stabat Mater," in *Histoires d'Amour* (Paris: Editions de Noël, 1983).

5. Clément, "La Coupable," p. 7.

6. Ibid.

7. Ibid., pp. 7–8, and Kristeva, "Stabat Mater."

8. François Choay, "La ville et le domaine bâti comme corps," in *Nouvelle Revue de Psychanalyse No. 9* (Paris: Editions Gallimard, 1974).

9. See D. Agrest, "Design versus Non-Design," this volume.

10. Vitruvius, *The Ten Books of Architecture*, trans. Morris Hicky Morgan (New York: Dover, 1960). Originally published by Harvard University Press, 1914.

11. Ibid.

12. Leon Battista Alberti, *Ten Books on Architecture* (1485). Reprint from the Leoni Edition of 1755, with the addition of the "Life" from the 1734 edition. Ed. Joseph Rykwert (London: Alex Tiranti, 1965), p. 13.

13. Ibid., p. 195.

14. "You have seen briefly the measures, understood their names and sources, their qualities and forms. I told you they were called by their Greek names, Doric, Ionic and Corinthian. The Doric I told you is the one of major quality; the Corinthian is in the middle, the Ionic is the smallest for the reasons alleged by the architect Vitruvius in his book, [where] he shows how they were in the times of the emperor Octavian. In these modes the Doric, Ionic and Corinthian corresponded in measure to the form or, better, to the quality of the form to which they are proportioned. As the building is derived from man, his measures, qualities, form and proportions, so the column also derived from the nude man and fluted from that well-dressed young woman, as we have said. Both are derived from the form of man. Since this is so, they take their qualities, form and measure from man. The qualities, or better Ionic, Doric and Corinthian, are three, that is large, medium and small forms. They should be formed, proportioned and measured according to their quality. Since man is the measure of all, the column should be measured and proportioned to his form." Filarete, *Treatise on Architecture* (1461–1463). Translated and with an introduction and notes by John R. Spencer (New Haven: Yale University Press, 1965), p. 12.

15. Ibid.

16. Ibid., p. 15.

17. Ibid.

18. Ibid., pp. 15–16 (italics mine).

19. Ibid., p. 16.

20. Ibid.

21. Francesco Di Giorgio Martini, *Trattati: di Architettura Civile e Militare* and *Architettura Ingegneria e Arte Militare (1470–1492)*, compiled and edited by Corrado Maltese, transcribed by Livia Maltese Degrassi (Milan: Edizioni II Polifilo, 1967), p. 4.

22. Ibid., p. 20.

23. Ibid., p. 21.

24. Ibid., p. 363.

25. Kristeva, "Stabat Mater."

26. Ibid.

27. Ibid.

28. This question of the relationship between Christianism, the church, and humanism is an entire subject on its own and should be treated at length outside the context of this chapter.

29. Kristeva, "Stabat Mater."

30. Clément, "La Coupable," pp. 7–8.

31. Julia Kristeva, "Matière, Sens, Dialectique," in *Tel Quel 44* (Paris: Editions du Seuil, 1971).

32. Jean Jacques Lacan, "Le stade du miroir comme formateur de la fonction du Je," in *Ecrits I* (Paris: Editions du Seuil, 1966).

Illustration Credits

All illustrations not listed are reprinted courtesy of the author.

p. 34 *Visionary Architects: Boullée, Ledoux, Lequeu* (Houston, TX: University of St. Thomas, 1968); **pp. 36, 37** Douglas Fraser, Howard Hibbard, Milton J. Lewine, eds., *Essays in the History of Architecture Presented to Rudolf Wittkower* (London and New York: Phaidon Press Ltd., 1967); **pp. 38, 39** Le Corbusier, *Towards a New Architecture* (New York, Washington: Praeger Publishers, Inc., 1960); **pp. 42, 43** Le Corbusier, *The Radiant City* (New York: Orion Press, 1964); **p. 44** Manfredo Tafuri, *Giovan Battista Piranesi: L'Architettura come "Utopia Negativa"* (Turin: Accademia delle Scienza, 1972); **pp. 45, 46 (bottom)** Alison Smithson, ed., *Team 10 Primer* (Cambridge, MA: MIT Press, 1968). Illustration on p. 45 redrawn by Jane Carolan; **p. 46 (top left and right)** Alison and Peter Smithson, *Ordinariness and Light* (Cambridge, MA: MIT Press, 1970); **p. 49** Sergei Eisenstein, *The Film Sense* (New York: Harcourt, Brace and World, 1942); **p. 53 (bottom)** Roseline Bacou, *Piranese, Gravures et Dessins* (Paris: Editions du Chene, 1974); **p. 81** W. Weisman, "A New View of Skyscraper History," *The Rise of an American Architecture*, ed. E. Kaufmann, Jr. (New York: Praeger Publishers); **pp. 82–85 (left), 89** Reprinted from The Chicago Tribune Competition publication of all contributed projects; **p. 85 (right)** Claes Oldenburg, *Proposals for Monuments and Buildings* (Chicago: ABIG Table Book, 1969); **p. 88** Alfred Bossom, *Building to the Skies* (New York, 1934); **pp. 90, 92–94 (top), 100, 101 (top), 102** Hugh Ferriss, *The Metropolis of Tomorrow* (New York, 1929); **p. 95 (top left and right)** *Architectural Forum*, June 1930; **p. 97** *Architectural Forum*, May 1932; **p. 99** *Global Architecture* (Tokyo: A.D.A. Edita, 1971), photograph by Yukio Futagawa; **p. 103** "The American Architect and the Architectural Review," *Architectural Review*, vol. CXXIC, 1923; **p. 104 (top)** *L'Architecture d'Aujourd'hui*, March/April 1975; **pp. 113, 115** Giulio Carlo Argan, *L'Europe des Capitales 1600–1700*, Editions d'Art Albert Skira, 1964; **pp. 117, 118, 122** Jean Starobinski, *L'Invention de la Liberte 1700–1789*, Editions d'Art Albert Skira, 1964; **pp. 133–135** Warner Brothers; **pp. 136, 137** Paramount Pictures; **p. 138** *Bergasse 19, S. Freud's Home and Offices, Vienna 1938—The Photographs of Edmund Engelman* (New York: Basic Books, 1976), Plate 27; **pp. 141, 144 (right), 145 (bottom)** Anthony Blunt, *Baroque and Rococo, Architecture and Decoration* (Harper and Row, 1978); **pp. 142, 143, 147** Athanase Kircher, *Ars Magna Lucis et Umbrae* (Rome 1646); **p. 144 (left)** Jacques du Breuil, *La Perspective Pratique* (Paris, 1649); **p. 145 (top)** Allan Braham, *The Architecture of French Enlightenment* (London: Thames and Hudson, 1980); **p. 149** *Progressive Architecture*, December 1974; **p. 151 (left)** *Progressive Architecture*, December 1979; **p. 151 (top right)** *Architecture and Urbanism*, January 1979; **p. 151 (bottom right)** *Progressive Architecture*, October 1976; **p. 153** *Progressive Architecture*, July 1979; **p. 154** Harry Torczyner, *Magritte: Ideas and Images* (New York: Harry N. Abrams, 1977); **p. 156** Diderot, *Encyclopedie*; **pp. 157, 159** Beaumont Newhall, *The History of Photography* (New York, The Museum of Modern Art, 1964); **pp. 160, 169** *Places and Memories: Photographs by Roberto Schezen* (Rizzoli International Publications, 1988); **pp. 161, 163, 164** *The Photographs of Eugene Atget, the Words of Marcel Proust, A Vision of Paris*, Arthur D. Trottenberg, ed. (New York: Macmillan Publishing Co., Inc., 1963); **pp. 165, 166, 168 (top)** *Man Ray Photographer*, introduction by Jean-Hubert Martin (Paris: Philippe Sers, 1981); **p. 168 (bottom left and right)** Andreas Haus, *Photographs and Photograms—Moholy Nagy* (New York: Pantheon Books, 1980); **pp. 175, 176, 182, 183, 185–187** Francesco di Giorgio Martini, *Trattati di Architettura Ingegneria e Arte Militare* (Milan: Edizioni Il Polifilo, 1967); **p. 178** Renato de Fusco, *Il Codice Dell'Architettura, Antologia di Trattatisti* (Naples: Edizioni Scientifiche Italiane, 1968); **p. 180** Filarete, *Treatise on Architecture (1461–1463)* (John R. Spencer, 1965).